The Perfect Puppy:

How to Choose Your Dog by Its Behavior

The Perfect Puppy:

How to Choose Your Dog by Its Behavior

Benjamin L. Hart
Lynette A. Hart

University of California, Davis

W. H. Freeman and Company ■ **New York**

Cover photograph: © Elizabeth Hathon

Library of Congress Cataloging-in-Publication Data

Hart, Benjamin L.
  The perfect puppy:
  How to choose your dog by its behavior.

  Bibliography: p.
  Includes index.
  1. Dog breeds.   2. Dogs—Behavior.   3. Dogs.
  I. Hart, Lynette A.   II. Title.
  SF426.H38   1988   636.7'1   87-8522
  ISBN 0-7167-1926-6
  ISBN 0-7167-1829-4 (pbk.)

Printed in the United States of America

Tenth printing, 1998

*To Joan and her very special
canine friend, Sid*

Contents

Preface

Puppies are such winning creatures that we can't help falling in love with them. But if you are thinking of adopting one, you should not underestimate the careful consideration needed to make your selection; after all, the puppy you choose today will grow into the dog that will be your companion for the next ten to twenty years. The purpose of this book is to help you, the prospective dog owner, select the breed and gender best suited to your lifestyle and environment. A hasty, uninformed decision might lead you straight to the pound, but carefully choosing a breed by using the information in the behavioral profiles means that you can anticipate a happy and loving long-term relationship with your new pet.

For those of you who already own a dog, or who have established breed loyalties, the behavioral profiles can still offer some useful information. Because we want to enhance your appreciation and knowledge of canine behavioral traits, we have presented the profiles in a readily accessible format of text and graphs. You will see from brief browsing that there are major behavioral differences between many breeds, and so there are plenty of opportunities to select the best breed for you—or to advise others on breed selection.

Let us quickly point out that the information does not represent our own opinions but is based on the rankings assigned by a large number of small-animal veterinarians and dog obedience judges. We firmly believe that no breed is better than another; rather, there is a wide range of roles, each filled admirably by different breeds. There is an almost perfect dog for any situation, and this book can be invaluable in helping you choose the best dog for you.

Through the years, many of you have expressed interest in learning about dog selection, and it is because of you and for you that we have written this book. Finally, we would like to acknowledge the interviewers, veterinarians, and dog obedience judges who patiently worked with us in ranking the breeds.

Part 1

Knowing What to Look for in a Dog

Chapter 1

How to Use This Book
to Select Your Dog

Let's say you've decided that you want a puppy, but you don't know what breed to choose. You may have really loved a Golden Retriever you once had, but a friend's house was burglarized while her Retriever simply wagged his tail and looked on. A dog breeder you know claims that Standard Poodles are the best all-around breed, and a neighbor swears by Dobermans. Your cousin says to stay away from Beagles—unless you like to hear barking all night.

Whose opinion should you trust? Can anyone really know enough about all the different breeds to let you base your selection on a single person's advice? And how can you evaluate all the books that discuss the good points of the various breeds? The problem is that no one person can be the sole authority on all breeds. Breeders may have a bias, or at least loyalty, toward their own breeds. Likewise, authors writing about certain breeds may have their own biases.

Authorities on dogs are frequently asked, "What is the best breed of dog?" This question is impossible to answer, because there is no "best" breed. Different breeds are suited for different environments. The breed or group of breeds that might be ideal for a young man living alone who is away at work every day is different from the breed that would be ideal for a family with children who would frequently play with the dog in a large backyard. The best breed for a person in a crime-ridden neighborhood may not be the best breed for someone who lives where there is less crime.

The Perfect Puppy: How to Choose Your Dog by Its Behavior is a data-based, scientific approach to describing the behavioral differences between breeds that shows you how to evaluate these factors in selecting a puppy. The scientific rationale and methodology of the study that provided the information here have been published in a professional journal (Hart and Miller, 1985; Hart and Hart, 1985a).

3

Most of the information here about the different breeds concerns behavior, which is what prospective dog owners are most interested in. This information is scientifically accurate, but in a readily understandable form. Naturally, people choose a breed because of its size, coat, or distinctive coloration. But the main reason for wanting a particular dog for a pet is its behavior. Whether a dog seeks or is indifferent to affection or is easily trained and managed is generally more important than, say, its size.

There is a great deal of variability among individual dogs within any particular breed, which has to be taken into account when comparing breeds. This range limits the accuracy of any behavioral profile of a particular breed. Some individual dogs within a given breed are clearly going to come closer to our behavioral descriptions than will others.

Prospective dog owners should also seek out the advice of breeders, members of local dog clubs, and obedience trainers for their insights into the behavior of the various breeds. The advice and comments that most reputable dog breeders will make about their breed in comparison with other breeds will usually be honest and candid. They are generally in the business for their own enjoyment and love of dogs, rather than for the money. Although this book provides a practical approach to selecting a dog breed, it is nevertheless advisable to follow up by consulting knowledgeable people for additional information once the choices are narrowed.

Mongrels versus Purebreds

Most people who want a dog think about adopting a puppy. How can anyone make reasonable predictions about how a puppy will behave as an adult? For one thing, it is easiest to deal with purebreds in collecting and organizing information about different breeds. Mongrels are by definition the product of mixing at least two purebreds—rarely intentionally—so no generalizations apply equally to all mongrels. People often claim that mongrels are calmer and not as high-strung as purebreds, are better with children, less fragile, and so forth. The point is that if calmness, for instance, is what you want, a purebred of a breed characterized by low excitability is the safest bet. There is no way for people to compare a dog they know now with a mongrel remembered from childhood. Through the information in this book you can select breeds with behavioral characteristics that match your own preferences, lifestyle, and personal demands.

A particular value of selecting a purebred puppy over a mixed breed is in being able to predict the characteristics of the dog as an adult. By thinking of how a particular breed looks in adulthood, we can know what to expect as a puppy of that breed gets older. We know that an Irish Setter puppy will differ from a Golden Retriever puppy in certain predictable attributes of coat color and length, as well as body build. It is also reasonable to have certain expectations regarding behavior, such as the idea that the Setter is likely to be more lively than the Retriever.

Nothing said thus far is meant to imply that mongrels cannot make great pets. Millions of mongrels become ideal family dogs. Delightful mixed-breed puppies are often available from neighborhood breeders or animal shelters. The purchase price, if any, is usually no more than the cost of vaccinations. When a mongrel is an obvious cross between two identifiable breeds, as is often the case, you can certainly learn something about the dog's probable adult behavior by consulting the behavioral profile of the puppy's breeds. Particularly with mongrels it is important to inquire about the background of the puppy and the behavior of its mother and father.

What's in a Breed Profile

There are over one hundred twenty breeds of dogs represented in the American Kennel Club (AKC). The fifty-six breeds covered in this book represent only about half the total number of purebred breeds recognized by the AKC. However, the ones surveyed here include the most popular ones. These breeds are thus the ones with the most information available about them. The various breeds represent a wide range of not only behavioral differences but body sizes, shapes, and color differences.

The behavioral profiles for each of the fifty-six breeds in Part 3, from ratings by ninety-six experts, are for the most popular and generally the most frequently registered breeds. It should be noted that this system of ratings would not function with the less well-known breeds; information about them would be less reliable.

The authors' own opinions are not represented in the data. Thumbing through Part 3 will give you an idea of what a breed profile looks like. The graphs and discussion of each breed consolidate data into a straightforward, easily understood breed profile. Each profile also includes key information about the size and conformation of the breed. You can learn a lot just through studying the breed profiles. For instance, computer-formulated analyses indicate which other dogs have similar profiles. If, for example, you appreciate the lively spirit of the Irish Setter but feel that your studio apartment is too cramped for a large breed like this, you can look up smaller breeds with similar behavioral profiles.

In addition, through this book you can focus on particular behavioral characteristics and choose the breeds that are high or low on the characteristics you find either appealing or unacceptable. For example, a look through Part 2 will show the rankings of breeds on each of thirteen basic behavioral characteristics. You can see immediately which breeds are at the very top, bottom, or spread throughout the middle of the rankings for each trait.

A Brief Overview

There is, in fact, a best breed or group of breeds for your family and your home, but before discussing this list of breeds we must look carefully at what your environment actually is. It is important to look at your own lifestyle and the household setting in which the puppy you choose will live and grow up. In the past, people have been too concerned with the size of a dog and not enough with the dog's behavioral tendencies and how well these traits match the particular environment and lifestyle of the owner. Chapter 2 is designed to help you come up with a list of these key behavioral traits in your own order or priority. Then there is concrete information to use when considering the rankings on traits and behavioral profiles in later chapters.

In Chapter 3, you will learn how to interpret the distinctions between male and female dogs and see how to use these differences to advantage as they relate to the characteristics of different breeds. Male dogs contrast with females on ten of the thirteen behavioral traits discussed. For example, male dogs vary from females in their greater tendency to try to exert dominance over their owners and in their degree of aggression toward other dogs.

Chapter 4 gives guidelines for successfully raising a puppy once you have adopted it. Many of the most persistent questions are answered here: How can you avoid the problem of the house being soiled? What can you do to make sure that your dog doesn't dominate you or other members of your family? Should you have a male dog castrated? Would there be any undesirable effects on his behavior? Does having a female dog spayed cause her to get fat and lazy? Will allowing a female dog to have a litter before having her spayed make her more settled down?

In Part 2, there is a discussion of the thirteen behavioral characteristics used to develop the profiles of the various breeds discussed in Part 3. This part contains graphs of the thirteen traits, with each breed listed in order from lowest to highest on each trait. What to expect from a dog that ranks high or low on each behavioral trait is also covered. For example, although a dog may rank low on the obedience training trait, it is not necessarily going to be impossible to train. All dogs are trainable by nature, but some are more easily trained, especially in obedience. However, if obedience training is not a particularly important trait in a dog for you, you needn't really worry if you end up with a dog rated in the lower half on this behavioral characteristic. The thirteen behavioral traits were chosen to represent all the important areas of canine behavior, so by reading through them you can pick up a great deal of basic information about dog behavior in general.

The core of this book is Part 3, which describes the behavioral profiles of fifty-six different breeds of dogs. You will want to consult this part in detail after preparing your short list of dog breeds and after you have a proper grounding in the traits that are of particular importance to you, as discussed in Chapter 2 and more fully in Part 2. Thumbing through the pages in Part 3 will give you an idea how much information there is here.

Chapter 2

The Adoption Process: Choosing the Right Dog for Your Environment

Before you even begin to settle on a breed or short list of dog breeds, or decide whether to get a male or a female dog, you will probably start wondering about where to find the puppy and at what age to adopt it. This issue is preeminent in most people's minds, so let us deal with it first.

Adoption and Socialization

At what age should a puppy be adopted? It is generally agreed that the best age for adoption is between 6 and 8 weeks. A puppy should be socialized both to people and to other dogs, and there is a critical period, extending from about 3 to 12 weeks, during which the socialization of dogs occurs most easily. The 6- to 8-week age falls in the middle of this period. Adoption much before 6 weeks of age may disrupt a puppy's socialization to other dogs, and adoption after 8 weeks may interfere with its complete socialization to people.

In the socialization period, dogs learn to refine their interaction skills. They learn to become subordinate to people, which they must if they are to be in a household. During this period they also learn to show submissive and dominant behavior toward other dogs. They react to people more or less as they do toward other members of their pack. They crave social interaction and love affection and attention. It is thus dangerous for a puppy to be isolated or neglected during the socialization period. Such neglect often predisposes the grown dog to be excessively timid or, at the other extreme, to be aggressive as an adult.

What can you learn about the probable behavior of a puppy by watching the behavior of its mother, father, or siblings from previous litters? Because the mother dog contributes half the genes and is usually available for observation when you are selecting a puppy, most of your attention should be focused on her. Consider whether the mother dog's reactions toward children, adults in the family, and other dogs are ideal. If the mother acts fearful or aggressive, can the owners explain this in terms of something that happened to the mother, or does this behavior seem to be a genetic predisposition that the mother might be passing on to the puppies? Try also to learn about the behavior of the father, either by telephoning the owner or, better yet, by observing the dog directly. Ask the same questions you did about the mother.

You might also inquire, if possible, about the behavior of dogs in previous litters from the same father and mother or at least from the same mother. If these siblings show the kind of behavior that is just what you are looking for, and the behavior of the mother and father is satisfactory, you have about the best genetic picture that you can put together of your prospective pet.

Ask also about the health of the mother and father and previous siblings, to ascertain that they are free of any medical problems associated with their breed. If you decide later on to breed your dog, this early checking will assure you of a reasonably good chance that your dog is free of these defects, so that you won't be passing them on to future generations.

Adopting an Adult Dog

Some people prefer adopting an adult dog because full-grown dogs don't have to go through the chewing stage that puppies do or have to undergo housebreaking. However, adopting an adult dog has its own pitfalls. A full-grown dog may not adapt to your household as well as a puppy would. Also, adult dogs available through newspaper ads, supermarket notice boards, and the local animal shelter may have behavioral problems that you can't know about until you have had the dog at home for some time. You may discover belatedly that the dog barks incessantly, digs holes in the backyard, or chews up furniture. An adult dog from such a source may also be suppressing fear-related aggressive behavior that won't be displayed until you happen to present the appropriate stimulus.

These warnings about adopting an adult dog are not intended to imply that doing so won't work much of the time. Someone who is considering adopting an adult dog should simply be well acquainted

9

with its behavior. Ideally, observe the dog in its home environment while it is interacting with members of the household. If the dog in its normal home looks like the kind that you would like to have in your own home, you are probably safe in adopting it. Many adult dogs are available for adoption at animal shelters. The problem with such dogs is that you can't observe them in their homes. However, you may feel that shelters are the best place for you to obtain a dog. If so, consider two suggestions. One is to adopt a dog from a place where the shelter's personnel have obtained information about the dog's previous history or conducted some behavioral tests. Some shelters make this information available to prospective owners. Alternatively, you could adopt the dog on a temporary basis, getting everyone in your family and the animal shelter to agree that this is a trial. After about a week's time, you should know if the dog is going to confront you with serious problems. Meanwhile, allow the dog to experience the full range of stimuli in its new environment, possibly including exposure to children from outside the home, letter carriers, and meter readers. Take it on automobile rides and on trips which are likely to be difficult later on, such as to the veterinarian. A word of caution: An estimated one-fourth to one-half of the adult dogs available for adoption at animal shelters are there because they have serious behavioral problems (Arkow and Dow, 1984). You risk adopting a dog with problems if you go this route.

Sources for Puppies

It is no secret that the ideal source of a puppy is a healthy litter, raised by an attentive mother, in a household where good nutrition and kind treatment are the rule. You can then focus on the breed of the puppy and its gender. If the puppy's mother shows signs of not being adequately cared for, it is likely that the puppy itself has not been treated well either. For all the appeal that rescuing a neglected puppy from mistreatment may have, this type of pet is a poor risk. The malnutrition and lack of kind and gentle treatment may be reflected later in the behavior of such a dog as an adult.

It seems that children have a special attraction to the runt of a litter. Most runts admittedly turn out fine, but runts stand a greater chance of having future emotional problems than the more normal puppies from the litter do. There is also the possibility of undernutrition in a runt, since it is less able to compete for food than its littermates. A runt is also likely to have been harassed by its littermates, which may have enduring effects on its behavior if this treatment occurred very early in life.

The problems obtaining puppies from animal shelters sometimes also apply to getting them from pet stores. The larger pet stores may obtain their puppies from the huge breeding operations known as "puppy mills." Dogs from puppy mills tend to have been raised in an environment lacking adequate human handling and stimulation so the dogs may turn out to be excessively timid or aggressive when they are older.

When a mother dog disappears or dies within the weeks before her offspring are weaned, the orphaned puppies are deprived of important maternal interaction. In fact, regardless of the amount of cuddling that we may try to give, there is no substitute for the constant interaction the puppies would normally have enjoyed with their natural mother. What's more, the task of bottle feeding orphaned puppies is laborious, so a litter is sometimes separated for different people to take care of. The puppies' interaction with littermates is thus reduced. Experimental work on maternal deprivation has shown we can expect orphaned puppies to have a tendency to be excessively cautious, fearful, or aggressive as adults. It is worth thinking twice about adopting an orphaned puppy for a household pet if you want the best chance of having an adult dog that fits into your family most easily with no major behavioral problems. However, if you do choose to adopt an orphaned puppy, try to get one that has become a foster puppy of another lactating mother or one raised with its littermates together, so that it has had the continuous comfort and warmth of contact with them.

Choosing and raising a dog is a personal and emotional experience, as it should be. However, for a dog to continue to be a source of satisfaction and joy, it must be matched to its permanent household and environment. It is important to understand how your own preferences, lifestyle, and environment apply in selecting the right breed of dog for you.

To match a particular breed of dog with your own lifestyle and environment, it is helpful to use the thirteen behavioral traits listed on page 12. These traits are the ones upon which the fifty-six breeds in this book are scored. These traits are examined in detail in Part 2 to give you a basis for deciding which traits to focus on in selecting a breed. For example, you may not need a dog that will physically defend your house, but might like a dog that would bark at an intruder. A dog's effectiveness as a barking watchdog would thus be a central concern for you. Or you and members of your family might want a dog that is very affectionate, with its trainability being of relatively little importance.

When thinking about behavioral traits, keep in mind that certain groups of traits are related, like excitability and general activity, for instance. There is also a relationship between a high score on territorial defensiveness and a tendency to try to be dominant over the owner.

The thirteen behavioral characteristics used in ranking breeds

Excitability
General activity
Snapping at children
Excessive barking
Playfulness
Obedience training
Watchdog barking
Aggression toward other dogs
Dominance over owner
Territorial defense
Demand for affection
Destructiveness
Ease of housebreaking

The Home Environment: Family Composition

Probably the single most important element to stress in selecting a dog is family composition. The simplest case is that of a person living alone and working away from the home most of the day. Such a person may wish a dog that ranks low on the tendency to bark excessively and on destructiveness, but high on watchdog barking and ease of housebreaking, and moderate in its demand for affection. Whether or not the dog is likely to snap at children may be of little concern if there is never a child in the home.

The situation changes a bit if you are seeking a dog and are a single person presently living alone but planning on getting married and having a child within the next few years. A dog's natural life span is roughly 10 to 15 years, so by the time you have your baby you will probably be very attached to the dog. Before adoption is the time to give some thought to the eventual composition of the family and the nature of the home environment. In this case you would want a breed that ranks low in its tendency to snap at children and in its tendency to try to be dominant over the owner. Ranking low on destructiveness and high as a barking watchdog may still be a major concern, perhaps. You may have to compromise on behavior, however, to get a dog as low as possible in dominance and snapping at children. You will also probably want a dog that is not in the lowest group with regard to its general activity level or excitability, because dogs low on these traits tend to interact less with children.

In families with children, low rankings on snapping at children and on the tendency to exert dominance over the owner are usually important. We may find that a number of factors do not come immediately to mind, though. For example, most men exert dominance more successfully over a dog than do women or children. Choosing a dog because of its outstanding watchdog ability and territorial defense abilities may lead inadvertently to choosing a dog that also happens to have a high tendency toward owner dominance. People who are not particularly assertive with a dog may find themselves being threatened or snapped at to the point where it creates a major family crisis. Rather than be faced with a situation where you are constantly having to discipline the dog or else urge a member of the family to be more assertive, it may be wisest to select a breed that ranks at least in the lower half on trying to exert dominance over the owner.

A different home environment might have an elderly couple who are usually around the house and want a dog for companionship but are not interested in an overactive dog and would be uncomfortable with a highly excitable dog that barks and dashes around whenever there is a visitor at the door or the telephone rings. Such a couple might want a dog low in general activity, excitability, and excessive barking but fairly high in its demand for affection. Grandparents may well want a dog that also ranks quite low in its tendency to snap at children. Anyone especially concerned about not wanting to assert dominance physically is well advised to choose a breed ranked among the lower half of those breeds having a tendency to exert dominance over their owners.

The process of matching a breed with a particular lifestyle and environment should be clear at this point. There is enough variety in breeds to enable you to come fairly close to matching the interests and demands of practically any family and environment. By the same token, it should be obvious that there is no "best" breed and that for practically any breed it should be possible to find an environment and owner that would be well matched. Thus, the best breed of dog for a family depends upon the ages of the people involved, the assertiveness of the owners, whether they need home protection or not, whether they are usually at home or are often gone, and so forth. Obviously, the more thought you put into analyzing just what the environment is going to be, the more successful you will be in matching the right dog with that environment. The table on the facing page gives some examples of hypothetical family situations with the characteristics that might be assigned a high priority and their preferred rankings.

Home Size: Big Yard versus Apartment

The idea that big dogs need a big yard and that if you live in an apartment you need a small dog is too oversimplified. What should be a concern rather than just the dog's body size is its general level of activity. A dog that ranks high on general activity will typically require more exercising space than a dog ranking low, whether it is a small, medium, or large dog. To a small dog that is highly active, a house will seem perhaps twice the size as to a large dog. Small dogs can obviously get more exercise in an apartment than can big ones. The general rule that large dogs require a large backyard generally holds true more for the active large dogs like the Airedale and Irish Setter than for the more sluggish large dogs such as the Bloodhound or Norwegian Elkhound.

Of critical importance to owners wanting to keep a dog in an apartment are the traits such as tendency toward excessive barking, which is a disturbance to neighbors, the amount of hair shedding, the dog's destructiveness when left alone, and its odor. Some dogs, such as Beagles and Labrador Retrievers, have a stronger body odor than Keeshonds and Poodles, for example. The Doberman Pinscher has short hair, is fairly easy to clean, has little body odor, and is very low in general activity, so it could be an ideal pet for an owner who wants protection in an apartment. However, the Doberman is also

14

Hypothetical profiles of dog breeds for different households

Assertive single person or couple working during day

Characteristic	Preferred ranking
Watchdog barking	High
Excessive barking	Low
Demand for affection	Medium to High
Excitability	Medium
Destructiveness	Low
Ease of housebreaking	High

Nonassertive single person or couple

Characteristic	Preferred ranking
Dominance over owner	Low
Aggression toward other dogs	Low
Watchdog barking	Medium
Demand for affection	High
Excitability	Medium
Obedience training	High

Elderly retired couple living alone

Characteristic	Preferred ranking
Excitability	Low
General activity	Low
Watchdog barking	Medium
Dominance over owner	Low
Excessive barking	Low
Demand for affection	High

Family with young children at home

Characteristic	Preferred ranking
Snapping at children	Low
Dominance over owner	Low
Excitability	Medium
General activity	Medium
Playfulness	High
Demand for affection	High

a dog that is less easily dominated than are some of the other dogs also suited for apartments, which could be a cause for concern by owners who are not particularly assertive.

Grooming Requirements

The wolf ancestor of the dog obviously had to provide its own grooming and body care. Through the centuries, in breeding dogs to have particular coats, we have created breeds that depend upon human care for their best health and aesthetic appearance. A Poodle does just fine with no special body clipping—and, in fact, many owners of Poodles prefer them that way—but we are accustomed to seeing Poodles with a certain clip. Keeping up the typical Poodle look requires that the dog make periodic visits to its own beauty parlor or the owner put in a significant investment in time. The long-haired breeds naturally require more care in grooming and bathing than the short-haired ones. Some breeds probably require more time and money to be spent on coat care than on any other aspect of the animal's care. In the description of the behavioral profiles in Part 3 we list those breeds that require particular attention to their coat.

Body Size

The first thing that most people probably think about in choosing a dog is its body size. Some who want a dog as an extension of themselves may feel that a large dog portrays a more assertive nature. To others, a small dog suggests refinement and sophistication. To some a large dog is more huggable, but for others a small dog that can more easily sleep at the foot of the bed without taking up more than a tolerable amount of space is preferable.

There is nothing wrong with allowing the size of the dog to play a role in selecting the breed, but it is important not to accept some behavioral characteristics that are incompatible with the owner's lifestyle or environment. For example, most of the small dogs are of the terrier group, almost all of which rank high in excitability and general activity. They also tend to be high in aggressiveness. If what you want is a dog low in excitability and activity, choosing, say, a Terrier because it is small may be a mistake. It is not uncommon for the larger dogs to rank highest in terms of aggressiveness toward other dogs and in dominance over their owners. If you are fascinated by the large breeds but want a dog from one of the most easily dominated breeds, you may have to compromise on size. The size of the dog should certainly enter into your decision-making process, but you should approach your needs first on the basis of the breeds' behavioral characteristics. Then, after you have developed a short list of possible breeds, look next at the size of the dog and how much care its coat will require.

If body size is probably the first characteristic people consider in choosing a dog, the second is no doubt the sex of the dog, which we will discuss in Chapter 3.

Chapter 3

Differences between Male and Female Dogs

For many people the question of whether to get a male or a female dog is as puzzling and important as the choice of a breed. Fortunately, the sex of a dog does appear to influence its behavior in a number of predictable ways. Giving thought to a dog's sex as well as breed can take much guesswork out of the question of what a puppy's behavior will be like as an adult.

The main point to remember is that because you are looking at male-female comparisons using the same behavioral characteristics that make up the breed profiles, it is easy to see the interaction of gender influences and breed profiles. For example, selecting a female dog will not guarantee that the dog will have a low tendency to be dominant over you if the breed in general ranks high on this trait. Selecting a female will only reduce the tendency of this behavior to somewhere below the ranking of the overall breed on this trait. Likewise, selecting a female from a breed already low on the dominance scale will probably have little additional impact on the behavior.

The graph on the facing page will help you get some idea of the differences between male and female dogs. To gain the full benefit from the graph and the other information provided, review the background data below, noting the suggestions for using the graph to select the dog most ideally matched to your household and lifestyle.

Sexually Dimorphic Behavioral Patterns

When anatomical, physiological, or behavioral traits differ between sexes, they are said to be sexually dimorphic. Dogs are not very sexually dimorphic in body size or conformation, though males usually

18

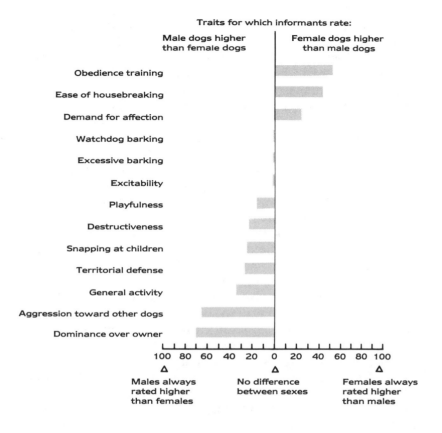

Traits for which informants rate:

| Male dogs higher than female dogs | Female dogs higher than male dogs |

Obedience training
Ease of housebreaking
Demand for affection
Watchdog barking
Excessive barking
Excitability
Playfulness
Destructiveness
Snapping at children
Territorial defense
General activity
Aggression toward other dogs
Dominance over owner

100 80 60 40 20 0 20 40 60 80 100

Males always rated higher than females

No difference between sexes

Females always rated higher than males

weigh a little more than females. A dog's gender is not readily apparent until you see its genitalia.

Most species of animals, including dogs, however, are sexually dimorphic with regard to behavior. Male dogs tend to be more aggressive than females, especially to members of their own sex. Of course, sexual behavior differs between the sexes, with each sex performing in a manner typical of it. Males display the leg-lifting urination posture and engage in urine marking much more than do females. Males also do more mounting of other dogs—and of people, when permitted—than do females. These traits in dogs are what are called pronounced sexually dimorphic behavioral patterns. In an attempt to reduce such behavior when it becomes objectionable, male dogs are often castrated (see Chapter 4).

The choice of a male or a female dog can be based upon these pronounced differences. If, for example, you already have a male and want another dog, you can expect less disruptive behavior between the dogs if you choose a female for the second one. If you already have a female, you can add either a female or a male and expect less fighting than would likely occur from placing two males together. And if you don't want to have to worry about a dog's ruining your manicured lawn with urine spots, you should seriously consider getting a male, that will usually lift its leg on trees or fences, rather than a female, that will characteristically urinate in puddles, creating pockmarks of dead grass. Finally, if you have had trouble before with a male dog repeatedly attempting to mount children or even inanimate household objects, you might want to select a female dog to reduce the chances of this problem still further.

Some of the sexually dimorphic characteristics are not so obvious to the casual observer of canine behavior. How much of an influence does gender have on the behavioral characteristics covered in the breed profiles? The sex differences within these characteristics are generally more subtle than the differences in urination behavior or sexual behavior, but they seem great enough to warrant the consideration of gender when searching for an ideal pet.

When interviewing the small-animal veterinarians and obedience judges chosen, we asked these authorities to state whether they felt that males or females in general would rank higher on each characteristic, or to say whether there seemed to be no difference between the sexes. According to the responses of the authorities we interviewed, whether a dog is a male or a female appears to affect all the characteristics listed in the breed profiles except the three tendencies toward excitability, excessive barking, and watchdog barking. For these three traits the degree of difference between males and females was so small as to be trivial and might easily have been due to chance.

Where a sex difference on a characteristic is indicated by a bar extending to the left or right, a significantly higher proportion of the authorities interviewed ranked male or female dogs higher than the opposite sex. The longer the bar, the greater was the agreement among the authorities that one sex exceeds the other. And the greater the agreement, the more pronounced is the actual sexual dimorphism of the trait, presumably. For example, if we had asked the informants to rate male and female dogs on use of the leg lift in their urination posture, they would probably all agree that use of this posture was definitely a male behavior, so the bar would be very close to the 100 mark. In comparison, in the graph at the beginning of this chapter, the characteristic with the greatest magnitude—dominance over owner—reached only the 70 mark. Surprisingly, at least to us, there were no traits on which men informants differed from women informants.

The relevance to you of sexual dimorphism in behavioral characteristics depends on the behavioral profile of the dog breed you are examining and what you consider an ideal configuration of behavioral characteristics. If the breed in question is high in destructiveness, for example, choosing a female might reduce the impact of this behavioral characteristic. However, if the breed is low on this trait, the choice of a male or female would probably have no impact on destructiveness, so your choice of gender should be based upon other traits in this case. The tendency to exert dominance over the owner might deserve serious attention if the breed ranks high in this trait but you are attracted to it for other reasons. Choosing a female of this breed could improve your relationship with the dog considerably. In breeds low in dominance, however, gender probably has only a minor impact, if any. Further, you can boost territorial defense in breeds weak in this trait by choosing a male of the breed.

We recommend that you first choose a breed that approximates the profile you like, then choose a male or female to enhance or attenuate certain traits. The choice of gender might alter the breed profile in a direction more favorable for your lifestyle or household.

The question of the effects of castration on the various breed profiles, especially on those characteristics rated quite high on the male side, is dealt with in the next chapter. One should choose a pet dog first on the basis of its breed profile, then with regard to how gender influences behavior, and only then think of castration as a means of further shaping the behavior of males if necessary.

Chapter 4

Raising Dogs

It might seem by this point in the book that selecting the most appropriate breed is almost the only thing you have to worry about, but this is certainly not the case. Not only is there considerable variation between individual dogs within the same breed, but many factors influence a dog's behavior, from its early experiences to the environment in which it lives as an adult. There are six major factors that influence the behavior of a dog:

1 Its breed
2 Whether it is a male or a female
3 Its individual genetic makeup within the breed, acquired from its father and mother
4 The source of the puppy and its experience in interacting with its mother, littermates, and with the breeder's family
5 Whether it is spayed or castrated
6 Its training and environment as a puppy and adult

In this chapter we will deal with the final two items, which are important to know about in raising your puppy once you have selected it.

Whether to Spay or Castrate

Most of the behavioral traits for which we have found differences among the various breeds also differ between males and females, as was suggested in Chapter 3. Castrating a male dog is likely to have certain influences on specific behavioral traits. The following changes are those you can particularly expect to see following castration:

- Less aggression toward other male dogs
- Less inclination to try to be dominant over the owner
- Less urine marking in the house
- Less predisposition to mount other dogs or people
- Less tendency to roam for extended periods of time

Our best estimation of the likelihood that castration will alter these behavioral patterns is about 50% (Hart and Hart, 1985b). That is, a castrated male is about half as likely to engage in the objectionable behaviors listed as would a noncastrated dog. If a male dog is castrated as an adult after a problem behavior has arisen, you can expect about half those in which castration is effective to show a rather rapid decline in the problem behavior and the other half to show a more gradual decline (Hopkins, Schubert, and Hart, 1976).

From the information we have, it seems that whether male dogs are castrated before or after puberty does not have a great impact on the effectiveness of castration in altering their behavior. It is reassuring to know that if you don't want to castrate your male dog until you determine whether a certain behavioral pattern will occur, the chances of the operation being effective will be just as great as if you had had the dog castrated prior to the emergence of the problem behavior. Contrary to the expectations of many people, we have found in clinical studies that neither the degree to which a dog engages in objectionable male behavior nor the dog's age when castrated influence the probability of the behavior's being altered (Hopkins, Schubert, and Hart, 1976).

There are a number of behavioral patterns we would not expect to see altered by castration. Castration is not expected to make a male dog calmer, less destructive, or better with children, or to decrease excessive activity.

What changes might one expect in female dogs from the spaying (ovariohysterectomy) operation? Most dog owners have their female dogs spayed to prevent their coming into their breeding condition (estrus) the usual two times a year after they reach puberty. Female dogs in estrus usually move about more, vocalize more frequently, and often act nervous. The urine and vaginal secretions of females approaching estrus have attractants sometimes called sex pheromones that are undoubtedly noticed by males living in the vicinity of such females. There are stories about male dogs being attracted from miles away to a female dog in estrus, but these attractants are probably not as potent as claimed and may simply be picked up by a male as he treks through a female's territory.

If a female dog is spayed, whether during or after an estrous period, she will almost never display sexual behavior again. Females thus differ considerably from males, which may continue to show some sexual interest for varying periods after removal of their gonads. There seems to be some general feeling that the behavior of female dogs may develop differently if they are spayed prior to their first estrus instead of after it, or if they are spayed prior to having a litter of puppies instead of afterward. However, there is no evidence that allowing a female dog to go through one or more estrous cycles has any enduring effect on her behavior. The same conclusions may be drawn regarding behavioral changes that might develop in a female from her having experienced pregnancy and the nursing of puppies (Hart and Hart, 1985b).

Do castrated male dogs or spayed female dogs get fat and lazy? There is some evidence that female dogs may gain from 5 to 10 percent of their body weight over that of nonspayed females as a direct result of the loss of hormonal secretions from the ovary. This difference is not a profound one, and one can nearly always assume that weight gain in male and female dogs, regardless of their hormonal condition, is mostly a function of the amount of food they take in balanced against the amount of exercise they get.

Housebreaking

Much misunderstanding arises concerning housebreaking. When we housebreak a dog we are not actually teaching it eliminative habits, but simply relying on the dog's natural eliminative pattern of keeping its den clean. Most domestic animals, including cats, horses, and swine, will eliminate in selected areas away from their nest or resting area. Dogs are naturally careful about keeping their home area clean, a habit carried down from the wolf.

A great many dogs are probably housebroken in spite of their owners' attempts to assist the process rather than because of them. The problem is that housebreaking is a classic area in which people tend to be anthropomorphic. Anthropomorphism is the tendency to believe that a dog's behavior or thinking patterns are the same as ours. When housebreaking accidents occur, we assume that the dog knows it has been bad, so we proceed to punish it as we would a child, assuming it understands why it is being punished. There is just no way to explain to a dog that has eliminated in the bedroom why it is being punished. Some of the common punishments, such as rubbing the animal's nose in the soiled area or pointing to the mess and verbally admonishing the dog, undoubtedly hinder the process of housetraining rather than aiding it.

The trick is simply to take advantage of the dog's innate behavioral tendencies to keep its den clean and help train it to generalize that the entire house is its den. This area, by the way, is one in which female dogs have a tendency to surpass males in how fast they catch on, as we saw in the graph in Chapter 3. From a puppy's standpoint, it must be difficult to perceive of the entire house as being a den. If it explores the house, it may come to consider the living room and dining room to be logical areas in which to eliminate.

Housebreaking should begin by restricting the animal to one small room or part of a room. People often find that the expandable gates used to restrain the movements of small children are also useful with dogs. These gates can be fitted with cardboard, if necessary, to keep a small dog from crawling through the holes. From this cage or restraint area, the puppy should be taken outdoors as frequently as is feasible, especially when its tendency to eliminate is high, such as after awakening from a nap or consuming a meal. If this procedure is followed faithfully, the puppy will not eliminate at all in the training area and will tend to hold its bladder and rectum until it has the opportunity to eliminate outside. Unfortunately, adhering to a regular schedule includes getting up in the middle of the night. After the puppy has learned to keep the small caged area clean, it may be allowed some freedom in the house while the owner watches closely.

If the puppy cannot be taken outdoors frequently during the initial training stages, first train it to eliminate on newspapers placed inside its small enclosure—but opposite the sleeping and feeding place. When the puppy has become accustomed to eliminating on the newspapers, it can then be allowed additional space within the house, provided it continues to return to the newspapers and use them. The puppy may be allowed increased access to other parts of the house at roughly 2-week intervals. The newspapers should be kept in one location. When they are changed, place the bottom papers of the dirty pile on top of the new clean ones to provide an olfactory cue for the puppy to use this area for elimination. When it becomes possible to take the dog outdoors on a regular basis, take it out when the likelihood of elimination is high. The use of newspapers can then be stopped.

Punishment has traditionally been part of housebreaking puppies, but it does little to facilitate the process. If the puppy has repeatedly soiled a particular area, such as a certain spot on the carpet, it may be useful to administer a sort of aversion conditioning to that spot by tying the dog up several hours near the spot so that it develops an aversion to the soiled spot.

Training: The Use of Rewards and Punishment

There is one key thing to remember in training your puppy, or adult dog, for that matter: a dog learns new things or changes its behavior only if the undesirable behavior is punished or the desirable behavior rewarded. We can reward a dog for performing certain tasks on command, such as sitting, lying down, or coming, with simple petting, affection, and praise. You can also use rewards for coming when called, for sitting when strangers arrive at the door rather than jumping up on them, or for going to rest on its bed when people are visiting. For rewards you can use reinforcement such as petting or verbal reassurance like saying "good dog." Another reward is food treats, if given judiciously, especially foods the dog really enjoys, such as a piece of meat or cheese. It is not our position that using food treats to train dogs "spoils" them, because the treat may simply be phased out by giving it less and less frequently, while retaining the praise and affection. Most dogs learn rapidly and quite willingly if there are rewards, and in many instances punishment is rarely necessary. Praise and affection, and food treats, can be used to housetrain puppies, especially when they are taken outdoors and can eliminate in a desirable area.

Punishment can be thought of as being either interactive or remote. In interactive punishment, a person hits an animal with his hand or a rolled-up newspaper, shouts at it, throws something at it, or in other ways makes it obvious that an aversive stimulus is coming from the person. The animal clearly associates the unpleasant stimulus with the person giving it. Unfortunately, dog owners are frequently misguided about how to use interactive punishment.

Interactive punishment is indicated when owners must assert their dominance over dogs to maintain an acceptable dominant-subordinate relationship, especially when threatened. A dog's growling or snapping at you when it is not a reflection of fear is best met with force. Dogs are social animals that respond naturally to factors in a dominance hierarchy, and their growling or snapping at you is an indication that they haven't completely accepted your dominant position. In fact, insufficient dominance—one of the most common behavioral problems of a dog-owner relationship—often stems from a lack of assertiveness on the owner's part. As we have seen, breeds differ in the degree to which they display a tendency to be dominant over their owners. The tendency to be dominant also varies with whether we are dealing with male or female dogs. Thus, a breed such as a Shetland Sheepdog, which is very low on tendency to be dominant, may never need to be confronted with interactive punishment, whereas a Doberman Pinscher or Akita may need periodic reinforcement of the dominance position with a sharp voice or correction with a choke collar.

Aside from using it to deal with aggression, interactive punishment is usually effective on acts of misbehavior only to the extent that the dog learns not to engage in the behavior when the owner is present. It is futile to administer interactive punishment hours or even minutes after the misbehavior. There is only the slightest chance that the dog will make the connection between the punishment and the act, and punishment delivered inconsistently has little effect on behavior.

The most effective type of punishment for acts of misbehavior is remote punishment. One example is the remote-controlled shock collar, which includes a battery-powered capacitor for delivering an electric shock through electrodes mounted on the dog's collar. When the shock collar is used properly, the aversive stimulation comes to be associated with the act of misbehavior and not with the person delivering the shock. Shock collars have proven effective in controlling a variety of behavioral problems in dogs, some of which may endanger the dog, such as chasing cars and bicycles and running away when called. The main disadvantage of the shock collar is that a dummy collar must be worn periodically during training so that the dog does not make an association of the collar with the shock. Another drawback to shock collars is their expense. They also require some practice and familiarization with them before one can use them effectively.

Another type of remote punishment is the use of a water sprayer for small dogs or a garden hose sprayer for larger ones. The secret to the successful use of sprayers is to not be seen by the dog when you are administering the punishment. The object is to have the dog feel that its own misbehavior or the object to which the misbehavior is directed is doing the punishing. Remote punishment must be given immediately after the misbehavior, so staging some occasions for misbehavior when you are there to punish it can be very useful. It is also important that to the extent possible every act of misbehavior be punished once you decide to start a punishment program.

Finally, we are great believers in obedience-training classes. Nothing can substitute for the social interaction of dogs and owners, the support you receive from others and the instructor, and the gentle pressure you feel to adopt a training program in order to participate in an obedience class. Some dog owners love to go further than basic obedience training and compete in utility classes, as well as local and state dog shows. The most important considerations are to enjoy your dog, to have its behavior match your lifestyle, and to do everything possible for your dog to live a happy life as your companion. By giving careful thought to breed selection, gender, and rearing, you will most certainly find the addition of a dog to your household a fulfilling and rewarding one.

 **Part 2**

Breed Rankings on Thirteen Key Characteristics

The first questions often asked by prospective dog owners are what is the best dog for children, what are the calmest breeds, what breeds should be avoided because they are difficult to housebreak, and what are the best breeds for watchdogs?

The graphs in this chapter allow you to select the behavior of most importance to you and to see at once how fifty-six common breeds rank on each of the thirteen key behavioral characteristics. Before you examine the text and graphs, read how the graphs were constructed, the precautions for interpreting them, and the suggestions on their use.

How to Find the Behavioral Information You Want

The vague descriptions such as "good natured," "self-confident," "versatile," "not quarrelsome," "dignified," and "wonderful companion" that are found in most books on dog breeds are not very useful when you want specific information like a dog's tendency to be drawn into fights with other dogs or to snap at children when provoked.

In contrast, the thirteen behavioral characteristics used here to rank breeds are clear, concise, and unambiguous. Each characteristic refers to a basic behavior that can be illustrated by a specific situation. The authorities consulted for this project were forty-eight small-animal veterinarians and forty-eight different obedience judges, divided equally between men and women and from the eastern, central, and western United States. We asked these authorities to rank seven dog breeds on all thirteen characteristics, after which a computer program assembled the individual rankings for each of the thirteen traits into a graph ranking all fifty-six breeds. The description of each trait includes the text of the question used to arrive at the rankings. For convenience, the fifty-six breeds in each graph are divided into deciles scored from 1 through 10, from lowest to highest, on each behavior. Each decile comprises five or six breeds.

Remember that the graphs you will be looking at compare breeds rather than giving an absolute score for a particular behavior. For example, even Basset Hounds, which are ranked among the lowest on ease of housebreaking, can be quite sanitary in their household habits. A score of 1 does not necessarily mean an absence of innate sanitary habits, nor does a score of 10 indicate infallibility in this regard. The graph simply specifies that there is a range in this behavior and that Doberman Pinschers, for example, are a better bet than other breeds if you are really concerned about having carpets soiled.

It is well to remember that this point about relativity applies to all characteristics and breeds. All dogs are natural watchdogs, are basically trainable, respond to affection, and exhibit excitability, playfulness, and so forth—but in varying degrees.

How to Evaluate the Rankings
in the Graphs

Obviously, there is very little, if any, difference in the behavior of two breeds that rank adjacent to each other on the graphs, say at positions 35 and 36. One should be aware that two breeds even as far as five positions apart may not really be significantly different. Not surprisingly, the number of positions apart that breeds have to be on the overall ranking to be considered definitely different depends on how well the characteristic discriminates between breeds, which varies from one characteristic to another. A span of two or three decile rankings, or ten to fifteen ranks, is a practical guideline to differences.

You will want to know which behavioral traits are the best in predicting differences between breeds and which are the least reliable. The table below lists the thirteen key traits, along with their predictive values, labeled as high, moderate, or low. We suggest that the traits with high or moderate predictive values be used in your initial search for a breed and that the characteristics with low values be used for secondary screening, especially in ruling out breeds having extremes of traits. For example, the graphs on excitability and ease of housebreaking are both useful, but you will have better success in choosing between breeds on the basis of excitability than on ease of housebreaking. Training and environment have more effect on the traits that distinguish one breed from another the least, such as ease of housebreaking, and less on those that distinguish one breed from another the most, such as excitability.

Not all the authorities we interviewed agreed about the placement of all the breeds along the ranking scale. In a few instances men differed from women, or veterinarians viewed things differently from obedience judges. Cases in which the subgroups differed markedly are mentioned in the description of the behavioral trait involved. Even when a large number of authorities are interviewed with an objective research format, the opinions of one group may differ from those of another. The different environments in which men and women or veterinarians and judges interact with dogs may give them contrasting views of the various breeds.

Thirteen key behavioral characteristics in decreasing order of predictive value

Characteristic	Predictive value
Excitability	High
General activity	High
Snapping at children	Moderate
Excessive barking	Moderate
Playfulness	Moderate
Obedience training	Moderate
Watchdog barking	Moderate
Aggression toward other dogs	Moderate
Dominance over owner	Moderate
Territorial defense	Moderate
Demand for affection	Low
Destructiveness	Low
Ease of housebreaking	Low

How to Use the Graphs

In using the graphs as your initial approach to selecting the most appropriate breed for you, there is a logical sequence to follow. First, choose a certain behavioral characteristic as your top priority. Stick to a characteristic with a predictive value that is high or moderate. Make a short list of about ten breeds that are closest to your preferred ranking, which may be high, low, or midrange. You may then want to rule out some breeds by virtue of their size, coat, expense, or even a bad past association for you. Now turn to the characteristic that is the next most important to you and see how many breeds on your short list fall within an acceptable range. If there are none, you may have to expand your short list from the first graph. Keep in mind the predictive power of the graphs, as explained. Use the traits with low predictive values to rule out extremes. Examine other graphs to narrow down your list. So as not to eliminate your entire short list, keep using a wider and wider range of acceptability as you look at each additional graph. For example, by the time you get to the fourth graph you'll probably be looking for breeds in the upper, lower, or middle half. Finally, examine the breed profiles in Part 3, scrutinizing the individual breeds in which you are interested.

Here's an example of how a search might work. Say that the trait of snapping at children is a primary concern and you decide that the breed you choose must be within the lower two deciles on this characteristic. However, if you are also quite concerned about having a good watchdog, you might decide to select a breed from the upper six deciles for this trait. You would then list the Collie, the Australian Shepherd, and the English Springer Spaniel. If your third consideration is a high rank on obedience training, all three of these breeds rank in the upper decile or two, with the Australian Shepherd having top rank. You have thus identified three breeds for further exploration by looking at their individual profiles and reading about their size, coat care, expense, medical problems, and so forth.

It is important to reemphasize what we discussed in Part 1 about there being behavioral differences among individual dogs within a given breed. These differences are a result of particular blood lines, the behavior of the mother and father, and the environment of the breeder in shaping the early experience of the puppy. Individual differences are as important as breed differences. And, again, the setting in which you place a dog will also affect its behavior. If you live alone and are always home, your dog's behavior may become more

32

mellow than the behavior of others from the same breed. The remainder of this section forms the basis for your choice of a dog that's best for your environment.

Throughout the rest of this book we have used such labels as excitability, excessive barking, watchdog barking, and obedience training, which are no doubt indicative of more general behavioral predispositions. With the statistical method called factor analysis, described elsewhere (Hart and Hart, 1985a), we were able to assign traits to a general predisposition representing an underlying common element. Thus, excitability, general activity, excessive barking, the tendency to snap at children, and demand for affection can be seen as being related to the underlying element we call reactivity. Similarly, territorial defense, watchdog barking, aggression toward other dogs, and the tendency to exert dominance over the owner relate to an underlying element called aggression. Obedience training and ease of housebreaking are assigned to an element we label trainability. And playfulness and destructiveness are included in an element called investigation. The breed profile graphs in Part 3 include these labels as well as those for the specific traits.

Excitability *medium - Low*

Predictive Value: High

Excitability refers to how easily a dog comes alive or is set off by a stimulus such as a doorbell ringing, a vacuum cleaner being turned on, or a car door slamming half a block away. When we think of a calm dog, we are usually referring to its level of excitability as well as its general activity level, which is discussed next. The specific question we put to our authorities regarding excitability was phrased this way: "A dog may normally be quite calm but can become very excitable when set off by such things as a ringing doorbell, or by an owner's movement toward the door. This characteristic may be very annoying to some people. Rank these breeds from least to most excitable."

Prospective dog owners are going to differ about the level of excitability that is desirable in a dog. Almost everyone wants low-level excessive barking, and most of us would prefer a high level of acceptance of obedience training, but excitability is a trait that clearly relates to the particular household or lifestyle.

The small breeds, especially the terriers, rank the highest on this trait. The Bloodhound, the Basset Hound, and the Newfoundland rank very low. Because it's not easy to find a small dog that's not high on this characteristic, people who have an excitable dog may simply tolerate it as the cost of having a small dog. Of course, having a dog constantly buzzing around your apartment is much less annoying if the dog is very small.

Excitability, along with watchdog barking and excessive barking, is a trait that our authorities did not rate as differing overall between the sexes. Thus there is no way that you can expect to influence this trait by selecting one sex or the other.

The predictive value of excitability is the highest of all the thirteen key behavioral traits. What this means is that you'll have more success in predicting a dog's behavior from its ranking on this one trait than on some of the other traits that have medium or low predictability, so this is a good trait to start with in narrowing down your list of possible breeds.

One trait that sometimes relates to objectionable excitability is excessive barking. An excitable dog is one thing; a dog that barks every time it is excited is quite another. If you're concerned about too much excitability in a dog but prefer one of the smaller breeds, look for one that doesn't rank high on excessive barking as well.

Breed	
Bloodhound Basset Hound Newfoundland Australian Shepherd Chesapeake Bay Retriever Rottweiler	
Saint Bernard Golden Retriever Akita Labrador Retriever Great Dane	
Alaskan Malamute Bulldog Doberman Pinscher Old English Sheepdog Collie Norwegian Elkhound	
Vizsla Boxer Chow Chow Keeshond Samoyed	
Brittany Spaniel Welsh Corgi German Shepherd Afghan Hound Siberian Husky Standard Poodle	
Dalmatian Cocker Spaniel Weimaraner English Springer Spaniel German Shorthaired Pointer Pug	
Dachshund Bichon Frise Lhasa Apso Airedale Terrier Pekingese	
Shetland Sheepdog Beagle Miniature Poodle Boston Terrier Pomeranian Toy Poodle	
Maltese Chihuahua Shih Tzu Irish Setter Cairn Terrier	
Scottish Terrier Yorkshire Terrier Silky Terrier Miniature Schnauzer West Highland White Terrier Fox Terrier	

0   1   2   3   4   5   6   7   8   9   10

Decile rank

General Activity

Predictive Value: High

General activity refers to how much a dog runs or moves about without being stimulated, whereas excitability refers to its tendency to be activated by a stimulus. A very inactive dog may be too sluggish to be a companion for many people, especially children.

This characteristic, like excitability, is one on which prospective dog owners are going to differ as to its desirable level. Activity also relates to the particular household or lifestyle of the owner. Some owners will prefer high or low level, but most will be happy with a moderate degree. Because the predictive value of this trait is high, you will be more successful in predicting a dog's behavior using this trait than those with lower predictive values.

The small breeds—especially the terriers—are highest on general activity, and some of the larger breeds—including the Basset Hound, the Bloodhound, the Bulldog, and the Newfoundland—are low. Generally, people who want a quiet dog that will sleep a lot and not intrude much on their personal space will prefer dogs ranking low on this trait. The question on general activity that we asked authorities was: "Some dogs have a tendency to just lie around all day and some are just the opposite—always on the go, continually active. Now an extremely active dog that 'buzzes' around a lot would get on the nerves of some people. Can you rank these dogs from least active to most active?"

Usually, the rankings on general activity and excitability for a particular breed were close. Where they differ may be important for some prospective owners. For example, low excitability but above-average general activity is characteristic of the profile of the Australian Shepherd. This sheepherding dog has been selectively bred to have an activity and energy level high enough to herd sheep for long periods of time but not be startled by peripheral stimuli. The Shetland Sheepdog is of a similar mold.

Our respondents ranked males significantly higher in general activity. Thus, if the profile of an otherwise appealing breed seems a little high on this trait, consider choosing a female.

In case you're particularly interested in the Old English Sheepdog, you should know that veterinarians ranked this breed significantly higher (35) than did obedience judges (5), who felt the breed was much calmer. This breed ranked 15 overall on general activity.

Basset Hound
Bloodhound
Bulldog
Newfoundland
Collie
Saint Bernard

Rottweiler
Great Dane
Chesapeake Bay Retriever
Akita
Chow Chow

Labrador Retriever
Samoyed
Norwegian Elkhound
Old English Sheepdog
Alaskan Malamute
Keeshond

Boxer
Doberman Pinscher
Golden Retriever
Afghan Hound
German Shepherd

Maltese
Brittany Spaniel
Pekingese
Vizsla
Cocker Spaniel
Dachshund

Standard Poodle
Pug
Welsh Corgi
Siberian Husky
Dalmatian
Lhasa Apso

Australian Shepherd
Weimaraner
Bichon Frise
Toy Poodle
Shetland Sheepdog

Scottish Terrier
English Springer Spaniel
Airedale Terrier
Boston Terrier
German Shorthaired Pointer
Miniature Poodle

Shih Tzu
Pomeranian
Beagle
Cairn Terrier
Yorkshire Terrier

Silky Terrier
Chihuahua
Miniature Schnauzer
Fox Terrier
Irish Setter
West Highland White Terrier

0   1   2   3   4   5   6   7   8   9   10
Decile rank

Snapping at Children

Predictive Value: Moderate

Snapping is usually thought of as being a signal that dogs use to drive other dogs or people away, without biting them or inflicting serious injury. Often considered an expression of irritability, snapping is also a form of communication that bitches use to keep their puppies from pestering them.

It is natural to expect dogs to use snapping as a form of communication with people. Dogs will usually not snap at adults to whom they are subordinate. And with adults who are snapped at, it is usually only their hands that are at risk. With children, however, snapping can be dangerous, because a child's face is often level with the dog's head.

Centuries of selective breeding have attenuated this natural canine trait until dogs of some breeds now seem to be almost incapable of snapping, regardless of how much they are pestered. Yet however hard we try to train young children not to abuse or pester a dog until it becomes irritable, we cannot count on a child's always following instructions. Families with a young child at risk who still find themselves wanting a dog are therefore advised to select a breed that ranks low on snapping.

Regarding a dog's tendency to snap at children, we asked our authorities: "This question deals with a dog's tolerance for being poked, pulled, and handled by children, not always as kindly as we might like. Picture the prospective dog owners who want to feel confident that their dog, once it is an adult, will not snap at children. For such a person, can you rank these breeds from least to most likely to snap at children?"

Snapping is a characteristic that differs in prevalence from males to females, at least to a minor extent. According to our authorities, males are in general somewhat more predisposed to snap than females.

The good family or children's pet would necessarily have to rank low in snapping. However, other characteristics, such as high rankings on demand for affection, playfulness, and obedience training, and a low ranking on dominance, certainly enhance the profile of a good family dog. Snapping is one component of the overall reactivity, explained at the beginning of this section, and dogs that are low on snapping will tend to be low on other traits associated with reactivity.

Breed	Decile rank
Golden Retriever	
Labrador Retriever	
Newfoundland	
Bloodhound	
Basset Hound	
Collie	

Golden Retriever
Labrador Retriever
Newfoundland
Bloodhound
Basset Hound
Collie

Chesapeake Bay Retriever
Vizsla
Brittany Spaniel
Australian Shepherd
English Springer Spaniel

Norwegian Elkhound
Great Dane
Akita
Boxer
German Shorthaired Pointer
Keeshond

Irish Setter
Bulldog
Doberman Pinscher
Standard Poodle
Rottweiler

Shetland Sheepdog
Pug
Alaskan Malamute
German Shepherd
Beagle
Samoyed

Welsh Corgi
Old English Sheepdog
Saint Bernard
Airedale Terrier
Miniature Poodle
Shih Tzu

Siberian Husky
Boston Terrier
Cairn Terrier
Dachshund
Weimaraner

Bichon Frise
Lhasa Apso
Dalmatian
Silky Terrier
Afghan Hound
Cocker Spaniel

Toy Poodle
Maltese
Fox Terrier
Chihuahua
Pekingese

Scottish Terrier
Miniature Schnauzer
West Highland White Terrier
Chow Chow
Yorkshire Terrier
Pomeranian

0   1   2   3   4   5   6   7   8   9   10
Decile rank

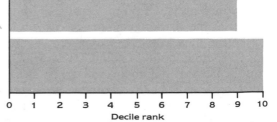

39

Excessive Barking

Predictive Value: Moderate

Excessive barking is an important behavioral consideration from the standpoint of responsible dog ownership as well as for your own satisfaction with a pet. Many people whose dogs bark excessively seem to be only mildly bothered by the noise, but their neighbors may be driven nearly crazy. Some communities have ordinances requiring dog owners to control excessive barking by their dogs if there are complaints. Municipal judges have been known to order owners to use antibarking electronic collars or even to have their dogs silenced surgically. (Watchdog barking, which is an alarm sounded upon the approach of a stranger, is presented as a separate trait later in this section.)

Dogs bark for different reasons, and excessive barking isn't easy to reduce by training. It is a type of misbehavior that's practically effortless for a dog to perform—few dogs tire from barking. Excessive barking, especially the barking that occurs in your absence, is very difficult to punish. Dogs may also bark when they are outdoors, if they learn that it pays off by having someone allow them into the house.

In ranking excessive barking, we asked our authorities: "People are often annoyed with dogs that bark excessively at anything, at any hour of the day or night. Of course, we know that large dogs have a louder and more impressive bark than smaller ones—however, aside from this, can you rank these dogs from the least to the most likely to bark excessively?"

Not unexpectedly, excessive barking is related to overall reactivity, which includes excitability, general activity, snapping at children, and demand for affection. Breeds like terriers that rank high on reactivity tend to be the noisiest. You can almost always count on a low-reactive breed to be quiet, but there are exceptions. The worst-ranked barker, the Beagle, is only average in reactivity, because the barking tendency in the Beagle was genetically enhanced by selective breeding to make it bark a lot while chasing foxes so that hunters could know which direction to ride. Our authorities differed about how given to excessive barking they felt the German Shorthaired Pointer was, with obedience judges considering it relatively quiet (rank 4) but veterinarians putting it up as one of the noisier breeds (43). The breed ranked about in the middle overall.

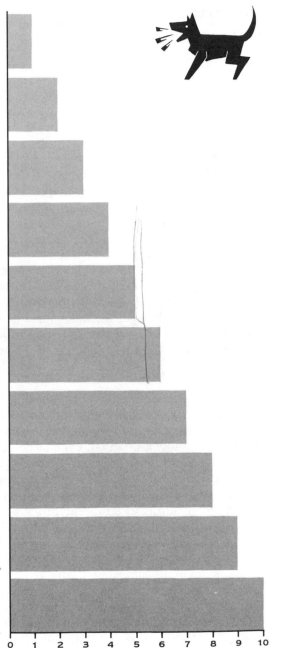

Breeds	Decile rank

Bloodhound
Golden Retriever
Newfoundland
Akita
Rottweiler
Chesapeake Bay Retriever

Labrador Retriever
Australian Shepherd
Great Dane
Old English Sheepdog
Alaskan Malamute

Saint Bernard
Boxer
Doberman Pinscher
Vizsla
Collie
Bulldog

Chow Chow
Brittany Spaniel
Basset Hound
Norwegian Elkhound
Afghan Hound

German Shorthaired Pointer
Welsh Corgi
Standard Poodle
Bichon Frise
Keeshond
Siberian Husky

English Springer Spaniel
Dalmatian
Cocker Spaniel
German Shepherd
Shih Tzu
Samoyed

Scottish Terrier
Weimaraner
Dachshund
Pug
Airedale Terrier

Irish Setter
Maltese
Pomeranian
Lhasa Apso
Shetland Sheepdog
Boston Terrier

Chihuahua
Silky Terrier
Pekingese
Toy Poodle
Miniature Poodle

Yorkshire Terrier
Cairn Terrier
Miniature Schnauzer
West Highland White Terrier
Fox Terrier
Beagle

0   1   2   3   4   5   6   7   8   9   10

Decile rank

41

Playfulness

Predictive Value: Moderate

A playful dog is just what some adults, not to mention children, need. Playfulness is one of the traits that contributes to a dog's success as a child's pet. Of course, all puppies are playful, which is one of the things that makes them such a delight. But as most dogs mature they lose their puppylike playfulness. Whether by design or unintentionally, though, the developers of some breeds have programmed into their selective breeding processes an emphasis on puppylike playfulness that remains in the adult dogs. It is possible to select a breed in which the dogs tend not to grow out of being playful.

We asked our authorities the following question about playfulness: "This question deals with playfulness of dogs as adults. Some people find playfulness desirable and others do not. Consider the person who wants a dog that, even as an adult, will play hide and seek, chase balls, or catch Frisbees. How would you rank these dogs from least to most playful?" The breeds high in playfulness are a mixed group of small and medium-sized terriers and certain sporting breeds. Traditional family favorites such as the Standard and Miniature Poodle, the Shetland Sheepdog, and the Golden Retriever are in the top 20 percent in playfulness.

Playfulness was rated by our authorities as being more prominent in males than in females, but the gender difference is not pronounced, so don't count on selecting a male to make much of a difference in a breed already low on playfulness. Playfulness is moderate in predictive value, so if this trait is important to you, you can expect some success when using it as one of your initial screening traits.

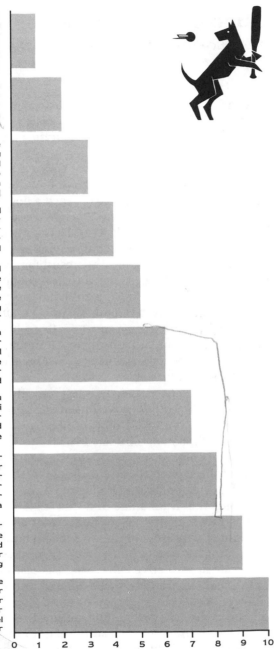

Bloodhound
Bulldog
Chow Chow
Basset Hound
Saint Bernard
Alaskan Malamute

Akita
Pekingese
Rottweiler
Chihuahua
Samoyed

Great Dane
Old English Sheepdog
Newfoundland
Lhasa Apso
Pomeranian
Afghan Hound

Keeshond
Siberian Husky
Chesapeake Bay Retriever
Doberman Pinscher
Norwegian Elkhound

Brittany Spaniel
Collie
Beagle
Maltese
Pug
Boxer

Dalmatian
Scottish Terrier
Cocker Spaniel
Bichon Frise
Weimaraner
Dachshund

Shih Tzu
Welsh Corgi
Silky Terrier
German Shepherd
Toy Poodle

West Highland White Terrier
Yorkshire Terrier
Boston Terrier
Labrador Retriever
Fox Terrier
Vizsla

German Shorthaired Pointer
Miniature Poodle
Australian Shepherd
Golden Retriever
Shetland Sheepdog

Standard Poodle
Airedale Terrier
Cairn Terrier
Miniature Schnauzer
English Springer Spaniel
Irish Setter

0   1   2   3   4   5   6   7   8   9   10

Decile rank

Obedience Training

Predictive Value: Moderate

You can, of course, teach an old dog new tricks, and selecting an appropriate breed makes the job easier. With enough time and patience, all dogs can be obedience trained, just as all dogs learn new things each day.

The question about obedience training we put to our authorities was: "Some people just don't have the time to devote to training a dog but would like to be able to teach a dog simple commands such as *sit, come,* and *stay* in only a few lessons. Can you rank these breeds from most difficult to easiest to obedience train?" The bottom of the scale on the accompanying graph reveals which breeds are the closest to being ideal in absorbing their training. Two of the three best-ranked breeds are classic sheepherding dogs, famous for their capacity to integrate distant hand motions by the handler with their own decisions in moving sheep. Our authorities, half of whom were obedience judges, perceived these breeds as having the top potential for standard obedience training. The top of the scale includes breeds that are likely to take a longer time to achieve acceptable results.

Ease of obedience training is not indicative of general intelligence in dogs. No breed has proved itself superior in all types of problem solving, so no one breed appears clearly best in terms of generalized intelligence (Scott and Fuller, 1965).

The overall trainability of a dog depends on its acceptance of obedience training and its ease of housebreaking. These traits usually rank together on breed profiles, but this is not always true. For example, the Dalmatian and the English Springer Spaniel are ranked much higher on obedience training than on ease of housebreaking. Put more faith in the predictability of obedience training than in that of ease of housebreaking, because obedience training is moderate in predictive value, whereas ease of housebreaking is low.

In obedience training, breed differences probably override any differences between a young and an old dog. Another consideration, gender, is also important. Our authorities felt that females take to obedience training more readily than do males. Keep this in mind if you want to boost the potential for obedience training in a breed that is ranked only as moderate in this trait.

Chow Chow
Fox Terrier
Afghan Hound
Bulldog
Basset Hound
Beagle

West Highland White Terrier
Chihuahua
Pug
Pomeranian
Pekingese

Scottish Terrier
Yorkshire Terrier
Saint Bernard
Old English Sheepdog
Irish Setter
Dachshund

Samoyed
Lhasa Apso
Cairn Terrier
Weimaraner
Airedale Terrier

Maltese
Bloodhound
Silky Terrier
Siberian Husky
Boston Terrier
Alaskan Malamute

Dalmatian
Boxer
Great Dane
Shih Tzu
Newfoundland
German Shorthaired Pointer

Norwegian Elkhound
Cocker Spaniel
Bichon Frise
Miniature Schnauzer
Rottweiler

Vizsla
Brittany Spaniel
Akita
Welsh Corgi
Toy Poodle
Keeshond

Labrador Retriever
Chesapeake Bay Retriever
Collie
Golden Retriever
English Springer Spaniel

Miniature Poodle
German Shepherd
Standard Poodle
Shetland Sheepdog
Doberman Pinscher
Australian Shepherd

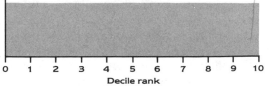

0   1   2   3   4   5   6   7   8   9   10

Decile rank

45

Watchdog Barking

Predictive Value: Moderate

Watchdog barking refers to having a dog sound a barking alarm upon detecting an intruder, whereas territorial guarding (discussed later) refers to the actual attacking of an intruder, even without barking much first. These two characteristics are often linked, but we have separated them, because potential dog owners often say that their preference is for a dog that barks at strangers but doesn't have a pronounced tendency to attack. Some owners may well have unannounced guests arriving at odd hours and will want to reduce their liability for unexpected bites.

The watchdog question was presented to our authorities as an imaginary situation: "A woman living alone in a city wants to get a dog that will sleep by her bed and frighten intruders by barking if anyone breaks into the house in the middle of the night. Rank these breeds from least to most as to which will most consistently sound an alarm when it hears something unusual and bark at intruders."

As you can see from the graph, some of the small terriers scored high on watchdog barking and some of the larger, less excitable breeds scored low. Thus there is some correlation between excitability, excessive barking, and watchdog barking. However, by careful selection you can find breeds relatively high on watchdog barking but not as high on excitability or excessive barking. Examine the profiles of the Doberman, the German Shepherd, the Standard Poodle, and the Airedale Terrier, for example.

From the dog's evolution out of its ancestral wolf pack, we might expect females to be just as likely as males to bark an alarm at the approach of strangers but to see males in the front lines for the actual defense of their territory from intruding wolves. This behavior is, in fact, what is reflected in the results of our query about gender influences. Our authorities found no behavioral difference between sexes on watchdog barking.

Bloodhound
Newfoundland
Saint Bernard
Basset Hound
Vizsla
Norwegian Elkhound

Brittany Spaniel
Bulldog
Siberian Husky
Afghan Hound
Alaskan Malamute

Golden Retriever
German Shorthaired Pointer
Old English Sheepdog
Pug
Bichon Frise
Cocker Spaniel

Labrador Retriever
Weimaraner
Great Dane
Chesapeake Bay Retriever
Beagle

Australian Shepherd
Collie
Chow Chow
Keeshond
Irish Setter
Dalmatian

English Springer Spaniel
Samoyed
Boxer
Pekingese
Maltese
Akita

Lhasa Apso
Shetland Sheepdog
Welsh Corgi
Toy Poodle
Pomeranian

Boston Terrier
Shih Tzu
Miniature Poodle
Dachshund
Silky Terrier
Fox Terrier

Yorkshire Terrier
Chihuahua
Cairn Terrier
Airedale Terrier
Standard Poodle

Rottweiler
German Shepherd
Doberman Pinscher
Scottish Terrier
West Highland White Terrier
Miniature Schnauzer

0   1   2   3   4   5   6   7   8   9   10

Decile rank

Aggression toward Other Dogs

Predictive Value: Moderate

A dog that basically gets along with other dogs is a more troublefree pet than one that must be constantly kept on a short leash for fear that otherwise it will tear into a neighbor's dogs or be a headache if you have more than one dog in your household. Of course, most people don't want a dog so timid that it slinks away from other dogs. Generally, however, the lower the dog is on the scale of aggression toward other dogs, the better.

The question about aggression that we posed to our authorities was: "Some dogs seem to get into fights frequently and others are quite peace loving. There are some prospective dog owners that particularly want a nonaggressive animal. For people like this, rank the breeds from least to most likely to initiate fights with other dogs."

The aggression factor as a whole includes three other traits besides aggression toward other dogs: watchdog barking, territorial defense, and dominance over owner. Typically, a breed tends to be high or low on all four traits. Examine the profiles of the Fox Terrier and Miniature Schnauzer for examples of breeds high in aggressive behavior, and look at breeds such as the Bloodhound and Basset Hound for examples of breeds that rank low on this characteristic.

Aggression is obviously part of normal social behavior for canids. The wolf with the more aggressive or scrappy temperament will most likely be dominant in its pack, but wolves that fight needlessly create unnecessary turmoil and wound themselves and others. In the process of domesticating the dog from its wolf ancestors, we have generally selected dogs that are less likely to fight and will at least tolerate other dogs that come to our homes or that we encounter on walks.

With this characteristic there is a pronounced difference between behavior in males and females with males much more likely to fight with other dogs than females. If the breed you prefer ranks fairly high on aggression toward other dogs, consider acquiring a female to reduce this objectionable behavior. Keep in mind that, when it becomes a problem, aggression displayed by males toward other males can frequently be reduced or eliminated by castration.

Golden Retriever
Newfoundland
Brittany Spaniel
Bichon Frise
Shetland Sheepdog
Bloodhound

Vizsla
Collie
English Springer Spaniel
Australian Shepherd
Irish Setter

Labrador Retriever
Shih Tzu
Standard Poodle
Cocker Spaniel
Miniature Poodle
German Shorthaired Pointer

Norwegian Elkhound
Maltese
Great Dane
Toy Poodle
Basset Hound

Welsh Corgi
Bulldog
Keeshond
Chesapeake Bay Retriever
Beagle
Pug

Saint Bernard
Old English Sheepdog
Lhasa Apso
Boston Terrier
Pomeranian
Boxer

Akita
Yorkshire Terrier
Dalmatian
Weimaraner
Afghan Hound

Doberman Pinscher
Pekingese
Dachshund
Cairn Terrier
Rottweiler
Chihuahua

Silky Terrier
Samoyed
Airedale Terrier
German Shepherd
Alaskan Malamute

Siberian Husky
West Highland White Terrier
Scottish Terrier
Chow Chow
Fox Terrier
Miniature Schnauzer

0   1   2   3   4   5   6   7   8   9   10

Decile rank

Dominance over Owner

Predictive Value: Moderate

The issue of dominance is probably the most important aspect of behavior in maintaining an amicable relationship between a family and its dog. A subordinate dog loves its owners and knows its position so it doesn't bite, threaten, or growl when given commands or discipline. The dog that's not completely subordinate may be lovable and even obedient much of the time, but it will occasionally express its dominance by growling, snapping, or biting when asked or forced to do something it doesn't like, even something as simple as being ordered to get off the owner's bed. Surprisingly often, small dogs—even lap dogs—are bullies in a household. To some degree this is a result of the reluctance many people have to correct the aggressive outbursts of small dogs, but it is also related to the predisposition of small dogs to resist being dominated.

The question about dominance that we put to our authorities was phrased like this: "As you are well aware, some people have problems with their dogs being dominant over them. This problem reflects the behavior of the owner as well as that of the dog, and size is often a consideration. Aside from these factors, rank these breeds from least likely to most likely to be dominant over their owners."

The wild ancestors of our dogs lived in hierarchical social packs in which dominance was achieved and maintained by physical force, but centuries of selective breeding have genetically manipulated the social predispositions of dogs so that some breeds are now usually quite submissive in their behavior. Being able to dominate dogs ranking low on this trait, like the Golden Retriever and the Shetland Sheepdog, should be no problem for even the most mild-mannered, unassertive owner.

Among the highest in dominance rankings are breeds that retain an ancestral drive to be top dog. The terrier group and such no-nonsense breeds as the Chow Chow, Siberian Husky, and Rottweiler must be dominated by their owners if they are to be acceptable pets. You may have to use a bit of force to assert and reinforce your dominance of these breeds. Dominance is one area where the dog's sex is quite important. If a breed's ranking on the dominance scale seems too high for comfort, consider choosing a female inasmuch as female dogs tend to be dominated more easily by people, or by male dogs, than are males.

Golden Retriever
Australian Shepherd
Shetland Sheepdog
Collie
Brittany Spaniel
Bloodhound

English Springer Spaniel
Labrador Retriever
Standard Poodle
Bichon Frise
Vizsla

Pug
Basset Hound
Newfoundland
Keeshond
Welsh Corgi
Chesapeake Bay Retriever

Old English Sheepdog
Miniature Poodle
Norwegian Elkhound
Weimaraner
Shih Tzu

Maltese
German Shorthaired Pointer
Cocker Spaniel
Irish Setter
Pomeranian
Boston Terrier

Bulldog
Toy Poodle
Akita
Great Dane
Silky Terrier
Doberman Pinscher

Alaskan Malamute
Samoyed
German Shepherd
Dachshund
Yorkshire Terrier

Pekingese
Boxer
Saint Bernard
Beagle
Cairn Terrier
Dalmatian

Chihuahua
Lhasa Apso
West Highland White Terrier
Rottweiler
Airedale Terrier

Fox Terrier
Siberian Husky
Afghan Hound
Miniature Schnauzer
Chow Chow
Scottish Terrier

0 1 2 3 4 5 6 7 8 9 10
Decile rank

Territorial Defense

Predictive Value: Moderate

Territorial defense refers to dogs' behavior in attacking a territorial intruder, perhaps with little warning. Some people live in neighborhoods where their personal property or safety may be at stake. They may even have been attacked already. In such circumstances people need a dog that will physically protect their homes and the lives of their family members.

We asked our authorities the following question about territorial defense: "Dogs are often owned in hopes that they will defend the owner's property by threatening or even attacking strangers that come around the house during the day or night. Naturally, the size of the dog enters into consideration, but can you rank these dogs from least to most likely to defend their territory, irrespective of size?"

Dogs ranking high on this characteristic are often high on aggression toward other dogs. However, they are also more likely to seize the opportunity to become dominant over one or more family members. For assertive people this should be no problem. For others, though, it is a bit of a trick to find a breed that is above average in territorial guarding but low in the other types of aggression. The Shetland Sheepdog, the Australian Shepherd, the Collie, the Welsh Corgi, and the Standard Poodle fill this need.

Obviously, the size of the dog must be considered in estimating its effectiveness in territorial guarding. Because, as seen, we specifically asked our authorities to disregard size when ranking breeds on territorial defense, you can find small breeds that are ranked high on territorial defense. The ranking of the Miniature Schnauzer, for example, suggests that this breed would prove a formidable challenge to any intruder. For the most part, however, intruders are naturally warier of a larger dog than of a smaller one.

Our authorities ranked male dogs superior to females with regard to gender differences and territorial guarding. If you are interested in home defense but the breed you are attracted to is not terribly high on territorial guarding, consider selecting a male rather than a female. And, finally, there is one qualification that must be noted. With regard to territorial defense, the Dalmatian was given a low rank of 6 by obedience judges and a high rank of 50 by veterinarians, although its overall ranking fell about in the middle.

Basset Hound
Bloodhound
Brittany Spaniel
Golden Retriever
Pug
Bichon Frise

Bulldog
Vizsla
Newfoundland
Irish Setter
English Springer Spaniel

Old English Sheepdog
Maltese
Cocker Spaniel
Beagle
Toy Poodle
Keeshond

Boston Terrier
Labrador Retriever
Chesapeake Bay Retriever
Lhasa Apso
Shih Tzu

Norwegian Elkhound
Miniature Poodle
Pekingese
German Shorthaired Pointer
Yorkshire Terrier
Chihuahua

Pomeranian
Collie
Silky Terrier
Siberian Husky
Dalmatian
Weimaraner

Alaskan Malamute
Standard Poodle
Shetland Sheepdog
Australian Shepherd
Samoyed

Afghan Hound
Cairn Terrier
Boxer
Airedale Terrier
West Highland White Terrier
Welsh Corgi

Great Dane
Dachshund
Fox Terrier
Scottish Terrier
Saint Bernard

Doberman Pinscher
Akita
Miniature Schnauzer
Rottweiler
German Shepherd
Chow Chow

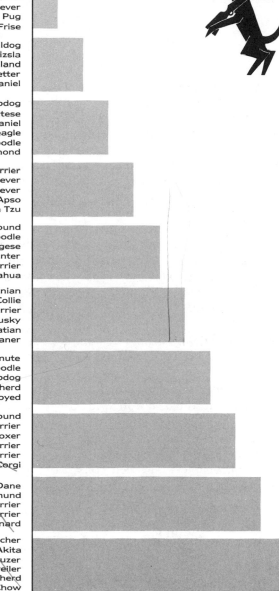

Decile rank

Demand for Affection

Predictive Value: Low

Puppies and juvenile dogs usually engage in much more physical contact than do adult dogs. This juvenile predisposition for physical contact has been extended into adulthood in some breeds by centuries of careful selection for demand for physical affection.

We phrased the question regarding affection in this way: "Some people would like a dog to be very affectionate and demanding of attention, while others prefer a dog that is much more standoffish. Could you rank these breeds from least demanding to most demanding of affection and physical attention?" In the rankings provided, the lowest-ranked dogs seem to be withdrawn and indifferent to people, but still usually obedient and subordinate. Breeds ranking high on this characteristic are more juvenilelike in wanting to be held, petted, talked to, or playfully jostled.

The demand for affection is one of the characteristics included in overall reactivity. The demand for affection is strongest in the more reactive breeds. But if you search through the profiles, you will eventually find dogs high in demand for affection that are otherwise lower in other expressions of reactivity. The Australian Shepherd is one example.

When children interact with a dog, they engage in a lot of physical contact and jostling, so a high ranking on demand for affection is desirable in a family or children's dog. Since our authorities ranked females higher on this trait in general than males, you can enhance this behavior by selecting a female.

Some people feel that their constant reinforcement of their own dominance makes a dog feel less inclined to be affectionate. Actually, it is the other way around: dogs express affection toward a dominant individual. In a wolf pack, the dominant wolf is sought out, and others want to be near it and display affection toward it. If you are looking for a dog that displays lots of affection, think about combining high demand for affection with a low tendency to be dominant over its owner. Because demand for affection is low on predictive value, it is best to regard it as secondary in deciding among several breeds.

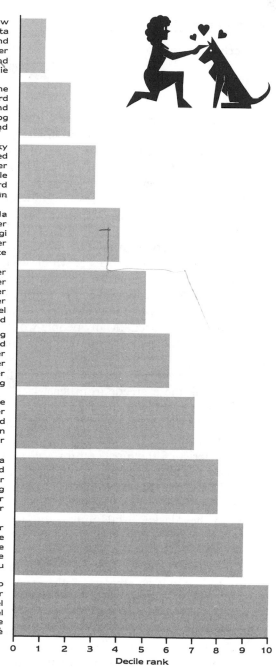

Chow Chow
Akita
Bloodhound
Rottweiler
Basset Hound
Collie

Great Dane
Saint Bernard
Afghan Hound
Bulldog
Norwegian Elkhound

Siberian Husky
Samoyed
Airedale Terrier
Beagle
German Shepherd
Dalmatian

Vizsla
Scottish Terrier
Welsh Corgi
Fox Terrier
Alaskan Malamute

Labrador Retriever
Boxer
German Shorthaired Pointer
Weimaraner
Brittany Spaniel
Keeshond

Old English Sheepdog
Newfoundland
Chesapeake Bay Retriever
Cairn Terrier
Doberman Pinscher
Pug

Standard Poodle
Miniature Schnauzer
Dachshund
Pomeranian
Golden Retriever

Chihuahua
Australian Shepherd
Irish Setter
Shetland Sheepdog
West Highland White Terrier
Silky Terrier

Yorkshire Terrier
Pekingese
Bichon Frise
Maltese
Shih Tzu

Lhasa Apso
Boston Terrier
English Springer Spaniel
Cocker Spaniel
Toy Poodle
Miniature Poodle

0   1   2   3   4   5   6   7   8   9   10

Decile rank

Destructiveness

Predictive Value: Low

We probably shouldn't be surprised if a dog's understanding of entertainment and destructiveness differs from our own. A dog's playing tug-of-war with a rubber hose is destructive as we see it if the hose is new, but a dog's chewing up of an old rubber hose that would soon have been thrown out anyway may seem to us just a cute bit of play. The same holds for chewing up new shoes, which is destructiveness, but if they are worn out it may seem to us merely a healthy gum and tooth exercise. It is difficult to define how destructiveness is sometimes understood in canine terms, but there are still some breed differences of which we can take advantage.

Destructiveness is generally seen as a necessary evil of puppyhood that is dramatically reduced in maturity. Our authorities were asked to rank breeds on the destructiveness of adult dogs, not puppies, to avoid this effect: "Many people would like to own a dog but are worried about a dog's reputation as an adult for destructive behavior. As you are well aware, many people must work or, for whatever reason, have to leave a dog alone for several hours during the day. Rank these breeds from least likely to most likely to tear up things either in the house or in the yard when left alone."

The breeds' rankings on playfulness and destructiveness are usually close together. When the rankings differ markedly between the two characteristics, the most comfortable arrangement for owners is low destructiveness and high playfulness. The best illustrations of this profile are the Golden Retriever and the Standard Poodle. The opposite combination—high destructiveness and low playfulness—is seen in the Alaskan Malamute, the Samoyed, and the Siberian Husky, which are, oddly enough, all sled dogs.

Destructiveness was rated by our authorities as being somewhat more prominent in males than in females, but the gender difference on this trait is not as great as with some others, so don't expect much leverage by selecting a female. Especially don't count on gender to reduce destructiveness markedly in the high-ranking breeds.

Because destructiveness has a low predictive value, it's not a good characteristic to use for initial screening. It should be seen more as one of the traits to use in narrowing down your short list.

Breed group	Decile rank
Bloodhound Bulldog Pekingese Golden Retriever Newfoundland Akita	1
Welsh Corgi Collie Keeshond Chihuahua Basset Hound	2
Rottweiler Vizsla Saint Bernard Labrador Retriever Shetland Sheepdog Chow Chow	3
Shih Tzu Boxer Standard Poodle Maltese Australian Shepherd	4
Toy Poodle Silky Terrier Boston Terrier Bichon Frise Norwegian Elkhound Brittany Spaniel	5
Pug Lhasa Apso Miniature Poodle Great Dane Doberman Pinscher Cocker Spaniel	6
Beagle Old English Sheepdog Cairn Terrier Chesapeake Bay Retriever English Springer Spaniel	7
Pomeranian Yorkshire Terrier German Shorthaired Pointer Afghan Hound Miniature Schnauzer Dachshund	8
Weimaraner Dalmatian Samoyed Scottish Terrier Alaskan Malamute	9
West Highland White Terrier Irish Setter Airedale Terrier German Shepherd Siberian Husky Fox Terrier	10

Decile rank

Ease of Housebreaking

Predictive Value: Low

Why are some dogs less fastidious about elimination than others? For that matter, why should they be fastidious at all? Canine elimination behavior is an innate or instinctual behavior that was shaped by natural selection to help reduce exposure to internal parasites and intestinal diseases. When feces were deposited away from their dens, the dog's ancestors, and especially their puppies, became much less likely to ingest parasite eggs or disease-causing organisms. A few parasites are much more injurious to puppies than they are to adults. Modern methods of medically treating dogs for internal parasites have weakened the natural selection pressures, allowing dogs with less than fastidious eliminative behavior to reproduce themselves. The result is considerable variability among dogs in how well they can be housebroken. Human differences in how we approach the process of housebreaking our pets also contribute to the low predictability of housebreaking.

Dogs, unlike goats or sheep, for instance, have an innate, genetically programmed tendency to keep their dens or sleeping areas clean. Even small puppies that are just old enough to crawl out of the nest behave this way. When we housebreak or housetrain a dog, we are simply helping it to generalize that the entire house, and not just a corner of it, is its den. Housebreaking also helps the dog establish habitual behavior regarding when and where it eliminates.

We asked our authorities to rank the breeds on ease of housebreaking in the following situation: "A young couple with no children want to get a puppy. They both work but plan to take a one-week vacation as soon as they get the puppy. They hope to have it housebroken by the end of the week when they return to work. Can you rank the breeds from least to most easily housebroken?"

Aside from the obvious personal differences in how effectively people are able to housebreak dogs, the high-ranked breeds will probably develop sanitary habits with minimal effort on your part. The low-ranked breeds can be expected to be significantly more difficult.

Most dogs appear to be housetrainable eventually. Because females are rated higher on this trait than males, if you're interested in a breed that happens to rank low on housebreaking ease, consider a female.

Basset Hound
Dachshund
Fox Terrier
Dalmatian
Pekingese
Beagle

Pomeranian
Yorkshire Terrier
Siberian Husky
Lhasa Apso
Chow Chow

Samoyed
Weimaraner
Bulldog
Cairn Terrier
Boxer
English Springer Spaniel

Afghan Hound
Scottish Terrier
Pug
Miniature Schnauzer
West Highland White Terrier

Boston Terrier
Norwegian Elkhound
Old English Sheepdog
Alaskan Malamute
Great Dane
Irish Setter

German Shorthaired Pointer
Saint Bernard
Cocker Spaniel
Keeshond
Golden Retriever
Chihuahua

Vizsla
Silky Terrier
Bloodhound
Maltese
Rottweiler

Toy Poodle
Chesapeake Bay Retriever
Airedale Terrier
Shih Tzu
German Shepherd
Newfoundland

Labrador Retriever
Shetland Sheepdog
Collie
Brittany Spaniel
Akita

Bichon Frise
Miniature Poodle
Standard Poodle
Welsh Corgi
Australian Shepherd
Doberman Pinscher

0 1 2 3 4 5 6 7 8 9 10
Decile rank

Part 3

Behavioral Profiles of the Fifty-Six Most Popular Dog Breeds

The collection of behavioral profile graphs that follows is the most important part of this book. Hence it is essential to keep in mind what these profiles mean and what they do and do not tell you. Remember that these graphs represent not the authors' opinions but the results of interviewing forty-eight small-animal veterinarians and forty-eight nationally recognized obedience judges. As explained earlier, these authorities were equally divided between men and women from the eastern, central, and western parts of the United States. Each was asked to rank seven breeds of dogs that we chose at random from a master list of fifty-six breeds, applying to each the thirteen behavioral traits examined in Part 2. These authorities were not allowed to include dogs of their own choosing, so the evaluations should be relatively free of personal biases. A computer program was designed to rank the seven ratings of all the authorities and then make a master ranking of all fifty-six breeds on each of the traits that were presented in Part 2. These rankings were then divided into deciles for convenience in composing the profile graphs.

How to Use the Behavioral Profiles

You will probably enjoy thumbing through the profiles to look at some of the breeds with which you are already familiar. You may want to compare how closely the behavioral profiles match your experience of individual dogs. Remember that there can be a great deal of variation among individual dogs within a breed and that these profiles are generalizations by authorities who presumably have seen many dogs from each breed. Your recollections about the behavior of a particular dog from a certain breed will thus not necessarily match the profile presented here. If you are an authority on dog breeds and feel that some of the profiles are definitely out of line with your own experience, remember again that these are not the opinions of the authors of this book but represent a consensus of the opinions of ninety-six authorities experienced with these breeds.

Breed profiles approximate the relative differences between breeds as regards the thirteen behavioral traits chosen, but don't take the graphs too literally. The difference between a breed ranking, say, 3 on a trait versus one ranking 4 is probably insignificant. You can, however, probably count on the differences in breeds that rank, say, 2 on a behavioral trait as opposed to 8. In other words, if having a dog that is high in acceptance of obedience training is important to you, don't reject a breed with other desirable characteristics that ranks 9 rather than 10 on this trait.

In a few of the profiles, some authorities differed from each other in a way that was statistically significant, as is mentioned in the discussions of those breeds. In most instances where your own experience differs from that in the graphs, the difference is usually a reflection of the variability among individual dogs within a breed.

When you get down to composing a list of dogs that are possibilities for adoption, follow the procedure suggested in Part 2 for refining your list of choices. Briefly, examine a graph of one of the thirteen behavioral traits there that represents your most important concern, like home protection, for example, as reflected in the graphs for watchdog barking or territorial defense. Then write down the ten to fifteen breeds that rank in the direction you want. In some instances you may decide not to choose breeds that are high or low on a particular behavior but ones that are moderate in it. Next examine the graph in Part 2 that represents the behavioral trait of second most importance to you and determine how many breeds from the original list fall within the range you have in mind from the second graph. For example, of the ten breeds lowest in snapping at children nine are in the lowest three deciles for dominance over owner: the Golden Retriever, Labrador Retriever, Newfoundland, Bloodhound, Collie, Chesapeake Bay Retriever, Vizsla, Brittany Spaniel, and Australian Shepherd. Then go to the characteristic third in importance. You will probably find that to hold the list to at least six you will have to keep enlarging the range of acceptability on successive traits until you reach a point where you are willing to accept a dog in either the upper or lower half of all the breeds represented on the graph.

After you have a working list of about six breeds, examine the behavioral profiles of the individual breeds in this part to determine how their overall profiles match your lifestyle and household environment. If you aren't happy with the profiles of at least a few of the breeds, you may want to start over again, using a trait of secondary importance and enlarging the list of acceptable breeds, then proceeding to other graphs with a somewhat different mix of breeds.

Included with the behavioral profiles are shoulder-height and weight figures typical of the male for each breed. Although these figures provide the approximate size for each breed, recall that many breeds come in a wide range of sizes. Further, in the larger breeds, the female is often smaller than the male.

Most dog owners are likely to get much advice from friends and relatives regarding the ideal breed. When this happens, we suggest examining the behavioral profiles of these suggested breeds and comparing them with the breeds arrived at by the systematic process of deriving a short list through the steps just outlined.

How closely the behavior of your dog as an adult will parallel the breed profile presented in this book is determined not only by its breed. Another factor just as important in determining a dog's adult behavior is the specific genetic contribution made to an animal by its mother and father. If the behavior of the mother and father seems to match the behavioral profile presented here, there is an excellent chance that the pup you choose will as an adult behave along the lines predicted.

Throughout your selection process, if a breeder expresses opinions about a breed that differ from the profile presented here, recall that you are hearing that one person's opinion. In fact, we suspect that some breeders will be unhappy with various rankings. No breeder is likely to be delighted about his breed being ranked highest on snapping at children or high on excessive barking. However, the way the profiles are constructed, with some breeds highest and some lowest in the rankings, is like a class of students taking an exam, in which not all students can get the top scores. There is a student with the highest grade and one who passes with the lowest. If you're looking for the absolutely best student, look at the top students. But if you care only about whether the students pass or not, the ranking of the students may not make any difference. Our philosophy in this book has been that different breeds of dogs are suited for different environments and that for each breed there is a particular environment for which it is most suitable.

Afghan Hound

The Afghan Hound is one of the most distinguished-looking breeds, which is no doubt the main reason people are attracted to it. The Afghan is not active enough to be a pest, nor is it extremely low on reactivity traits, like some other hounds, such as the Bloodhound or Basset Hound. Overall, it is moderately high on aggressive traits. The Afghan's high rank on territorial defense suggests that you can count on it as a guard dog. This breed is large enough and aggressive enough that its low ranking on watchdog barking should pose no problem, if property protection is a high priority for you.

The Afghan doesn't have the behavioral profile one might consider ideal for being around children. Its high rank on snapping at children and its low demand for affection are two prominent reasons behind this rating. As a pet for adults, the Afghan is for people willing to make a strong commitment to obedience training and to expressing their assertiveness over the dog. The Afghan ranks fourth highest in its tendency to exert dominance over the owner, third lowest on acceptance of obedience training, and has a high rank on destructiveness. If you're devoted to this breed but want to enhance the impact of its obedience training and lessen its tendency toward destructiveness, consider selecting a female.

For the owner who enjoys spending time working with his or her dog and doesn't mind consistently monitoring a pet, this breed may be appropriate. If you're not quite ready for the challenge of an Afghan, the Boxer is a similar breed that ranks more favorably on acceptance of obedience training and the tendencies toward destructiveness, dominance over the owner, and snapping at children.

Weight: 60 pounds
Height: 27 inches
Build: Average
Coat: Long, silky; regular
  grooming required
Color: Tan, black, or
  combination of both

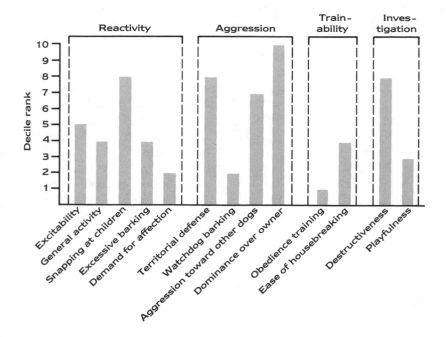

Airedale Terrier

The Airedale Terrier, though a fairly large dog, can be grouped with small to tiny dogs, many of them also terriers. If you favor the feisty, spirited terriers but want one with long legs to romp through fields with you, consider an Airedale. As is typical of terriers, the Airedale is quite high in aggressive traits but rather moderate on reactivity traits. Those who are fond of terriers but nevertheless want to get away from their extremes in reactivity, including excessive barking, may find the Airedale ideal.

You rarely find a terrier—of any breed—low on snapping and easily dominated. If your family members will be fairly assertive toward an Airedale, it would appear to offer a lot in home protection and as a playmate. The Airedale is within the top few of all breeds on both destructiveness and playfulness, higher than is typical for other terriers. One of the few terriers that ranks only modestly on demand for affection, you wouldn't expect the Airedale to pester you for attention, even though it is one of the most playful breeds.

Weight: 50 pounds
Height: 23 inches
Build: Average
Coat: Wiry, short; little shedding with regular grooming; professional clipping customary
Color: Tan and black

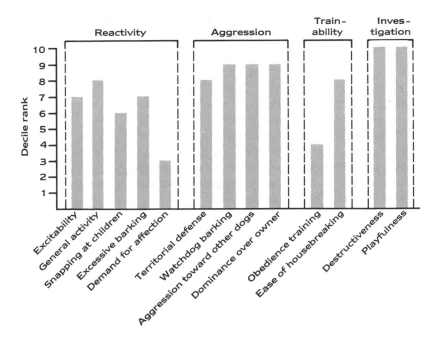

Akita

If you'd like a large, tranquil guard dog that is somewhat unusual, consider an Akita. Our ratings indicate that you can count on effective guarding by the Akita without having to suffer constant barking or challenges to your authority—one of the top few dogs on territorial defense, it ranked only medium in both dominance over owner and watchdog barking. The Akita's high rankings on aggression and obedience training are balanced by low ranks on the reactivity traits and destructiveness, unlike the somewhat similar German Shepherd. The Akita falls within the lowest few breeds on excessive barking, demand for affection, and destructiveness.

Perhaps you're a fairly small person who prefers not to risk getting a dog that might surpass you in body weight, but you're impressed by the behavioral profile of the Akita. You can get a somewhat smaller and less aggressive dog by selecting a female Akita. And if size is no issue, you can consider the remarkably similar profile and somewhat larger body of the Rottweiler. Both of these breeds have a manageably low ranking on snapping at children. To achieve reliable good behavior from the Akita requires conscientious obedience training, which should be rewarding, since it ranks high on acceptance of training. Your respect for the importance of providing discipline and some exercise may well be enhanced by the impressive size of this breed.

If you're willing to provide daily outdoor exercise for an Akita, you would not necessarily be foolhardy to consider having one in a tiny apartment. Its low rankings on excitability, general activity, and destructiveness make it a feasible candidate for small quarters, despite its large body size.

Weight: 85 pounds
Height: 26 inches
Build: Sturdy
Coat: Short, thick;
   odorless; no clipping
   required
Color: Various

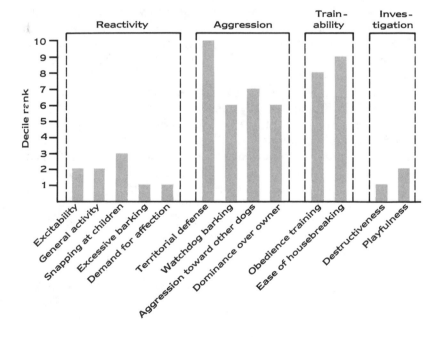

Alaskan Malamute

The Alaskan Malamute is larger than either the Siberian Husky or the Samoyed, two other similar breeds of sled dogs. As the largest breed of sled dog its level on reactivity traits is, not surprisingly, lower than that of these other two breeds. If you are particularly drawn to large outdoor dogs but need a quiet dog, the Malamute's low ranking on excessive barking and watchdog barking may recommend it to you. However, note its very high ratings on destructiveness and aggression toward other dogs, and consider whether you are prepared to insist upon obedience from this breed. Its ranking on overall trainability traits is the highest among the sled dogs, and its ranking on dominance over owner is only at the seventh decile. Thus, you might expect to be successful with this breed in a consistent obedience program.

The behavioral differences normally expected between males and females certainly appear in the Malamute and other sled dogs. With a female, you can expect to observe less exertion of dominance over the owner and aggression toward other dogs, plus greater acceptance of training. Should you consider a Malamute for a family setting, a female would be easier to incorporate into your home. The Malamute's pronounced tendency toward destructiveness may be reduced somewhat by selecting a female, but don't expect miracles. You might well want to consider inexpensive furniture or provide outside housing for the dog.

If you are thinking of a Malamute, examine also the behavioral profiles of the Siberian Husky and the Samoyed, because the profile differences among these three breeds are surprisingly slight. And if you favor this profile but need a smaller-bodied pet, think of two breeds that provide somewhat similar profile matches, the Dachshund and the Welsh Corgi. Rather than being low on reactivity traits and playfulness, like the Malamute, they rank at least a strong medium. On trainability the Dachshund resembles the low-ranking sled dogs, while the Corgi ranks high. Choosing one of these two breeds can allow you to reduce your pet's body size.

Weight: 85 pounds
Height: 25 inches
Build: Sturdy
Coat: Dense, medium
  long; heavy seasonal
  shedding
Color: Gray to black
  with white

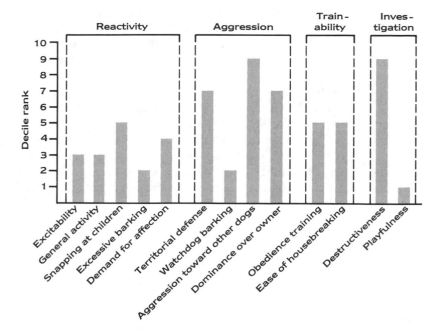

Australian Shepherd

You may dream of a dog so obedient that it seems to read your mind and anticipate your wishes, and one that would virtually never contest your or your children's dominance. The breed that would appear to come closest to this ideal is the Australian Shepherd, which ranked at the top of all the breeds for obedience training and second lowest for the tendency to exert dominance over the owner. Overall, this breed scores low on aggression but still ranks above average on territorial defense and watchdog barking.

The behavioral profile suggests that this breed would be a good choice if you want a benign watchdog. It will defend its territory and bark at intruders, yet not stir up a contest with you or other dogs or snap at children, according to our authorities. An owner wanting to strengthen the Shepherd's watchdog aspects could select a male and still not have to face an unruly contest of wills.

The Australian Shepherd's low score on reactivity traits is reflected in its having the fourth-lowest score overall on excitability and very low ranks on snapping at children and excessive barking. Yet the Shepherd ranks high on general activity and its demand for affection. The combination of high activity and playfulness on the one hand with low excitability and destructiveness on the other suggests that it is reasonable to expect members of this breed to be willing and energetic playmates, while still being relaxed and not high-strung.

If you favor the Shepherd's profile but prefer an even lower ranking on aggression, the Golden Retriever would be your best candidate. The profiles of the Standard Poodle, the Shetland Sheepdog, and the Welsh Corgi resemble that of the Australian Shepherd with respect to territorial defense, the low tendency to exert dominance over the owner, trainability traits, destructiveness, and playfulness, but these dogs rank slightly higher than the Shepherd on overall reactivity and aggressive traits.

Weight: 40 pounds
Height: 21 inches
Build: Average
Coat: Medium
Color: Gray, black, white,
and tan mixed

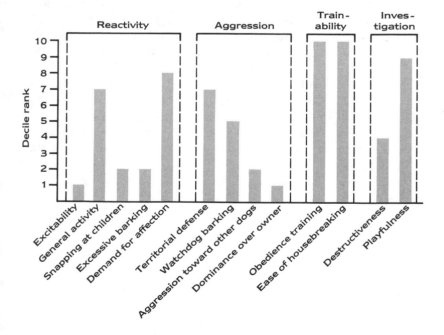

Basset Hound

If you must find a dog that is not active, excitable, or aggressive, the Basset Hound could be ideal for you. Bassets have the reputation of being a supercalm breed, and they scored the lowest of all breeds on our ranking for general activity. This ranking does not come without compromises in other areas, however.

The Basset has the lowest score of all breeds on ease of housebreaking. This does not necessarily mean that you will forever have a soiled carpet, though, for all dogs have the potential for being housetrained. But more patience and attention to housebreaking technique will probably be required with the Basset than with breeds that rank higher on ease of housebreaking.

The Basset Hound also scored lowest of all breeds on territorial defense. Very low overall reactivity, as with the Basset, usually means that the dog does not take well to a lot of affection and, as this breed's profile shows, you can't expect a breed that is low in aggression to be an outstanding protector of home and property.

If you wanted to increase the tendencies toward general activity and territorial defense of Basset Hounds, you could select a male. On the other hand, a female might well be easier to train and housebreak. A promising strategy for choosing a breed to moderate the Basset's lowest rankings would be to consider similar breeds that are stronger in those traits. If you'd like a higher level of ease of training, for example, look at the Bloodhound or the Norwegian Elkhound. If you want more action, the Old English Sheepdog is a possibility. And the Elkhound and Sheepdog rank higher on aggressive traits in general than the Basset.

Weight: 50 pounds
Height: 14 inches
Build: Strong
Coat: Short
Color: Black, tan,
    and white

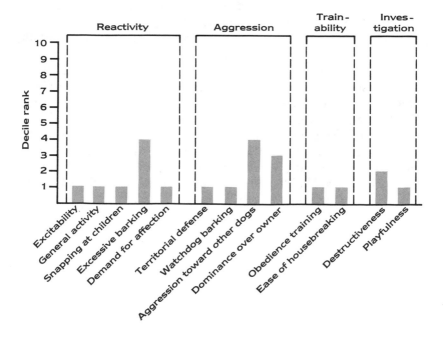

Beagle

It may be the distinctive, colorful personality of the Beagle that so endears it to people. If you ask a child to draw a dog, the drawing will probably come closer to looking like a Beagle than any other breed. In size, shape, and coloration, Beagles come across as the generic dog, which may account for their overall high popularity. Even their high ranking on excessive barking, which can be challenging at times for neighbors or adults in the family, is at least the very picture of what dogs do.

Despite the Beagle's lovable comic-strip Snoopy-like image, however, its behavioral profile suggests that it may not be the ideal family breed. The Beagle is not even strong on demand for affection. To its credit, the Beatle does not rank high on snapping at children.

By way of a further precaution, note that Beagles rank in the lowest decile on obedience training and ease of housebreaking. A rating this low is unusual for small breeds: only one other small breed, the Fox Terrier, ranked as low in trainability traits. Many owners might consider it unfortunate that the Beagle ranks low on territorial defense and watchdog barking, medium on aggression toward other dogs, and high on the tendency to exert dominance over the owner. As the top-ranking dog on excessive barking, the Beagle would probably not be the best breed for either a home or institutional setting.

No other breed is like the Beagle, but a similar and more moderate breed is the Pug, which ranks only low on exerting dominance over the owner. The Pug's overall scores come close to the Beagle's, but its trait scores aren't as extreme as the Beagle's.

Weight: 30 pounds
Height: 15 inches
Build: Light
Coat: Short
Color: White, black,
  and tan

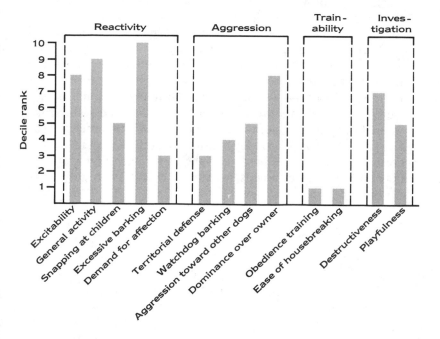

Bichon Frise

The profile of the Bichon Frise shows that it ranks fairly high on obedience training and low on aggression, so this breed may appeal to people who want a tiny dog with these traits. With most of the other small breeds—especially the terriers—you get a pet ranked high on aggressive traits and low on ease of training. This breed's high level of demand for affection makes it a good candidate among small breeds for a family pet. Notice, though, its high rank on snapping at children, which might require special preventive steps when small children are about. For a tiny dog, its modestly high reactivity traits and medium ranking on excessive barking are about as mellow a blend as you can get. As an added bonus, the Bichon Frise is in the top decile on ease of housebreaking. Between its tiny size and its facility in housebreaking, you should have no cleanup worries with this breed.

The Bichon Frise, which ranks low on aggressive traits, can't be considered a watchdog. If you're looking for a tiny dog with only modest aggressive traits but with high reactivity and a substantial aptitude for training, three other breeds—the Maltese, the Shih Tzu, and the Toy Poodle—have profiles similar to the Bichon Frise's. All these breeds are slightly higher in reactivity than the Bichon Frise. You might consider one of these breeds if you value watchdog barking, because they rank high despite their overall modest rankings on aggressive traits. The Maltese lacks the high ranking on trainability traits of the other three breeds, registering only in the middle on this factor.

Weight: 9 pounds
Height: 10 inches
Build: Very light
Coat: Silky, profuse; little
    shedding with regular
    grooming
Color: White

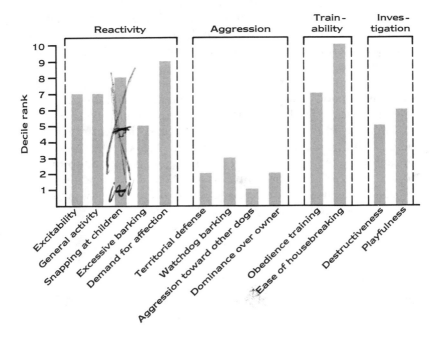

Bloodhound

The Bloodhound is a dog almost guaranteed to be calm and unobtrusive on virtually all occasions, yet be amenable to training. It won't disrupt dinner parties with incessant barking, nor will it jump up on your guests or snap at them. In fact, the Bloodhound ranks in the lowest decile on all traits except obedience training and ease of housebreaking. This unmatched record suggests that the Bloodhound's reputation for docility—for not attacking the criminal it trails, for example—is well-founded.

On a number of characteristics, our authorities were remarkably consistent in assigning the lowest ranks to the Bloodhound. In reactivity it was the lowest-ranked breed on both excitability and excessive barking, and it was rated the second lowest in general activity. In aggression it was the lowest-ranked breed in watchdog barking and the second lowest in territorial defense. And in both destructiveness and playfulness it was the lowest-ranked breed.

The Bloodhound's profile stands alone, even when compared with other breeds ranking low on several behavioral traits. Although the Basset Hound, for instance, approaches the Bloodhound in having a similar number of extremely low rankings, it doesn't have the moderate trainability that the Bloodhound has. Likewise, if you're willing to sacrifice ready acceptance of training, the English Bulldog is another breed to consider.

Because of its low rankings on aggression and snapping at children, the Bloodhound might seem a good candidate for a children's pet. However, other breeds that are rated about equally safe around children, such as the Golden Retriever and the Australian Shepherd, might be more ideal pets, since they rank higher on demand for affection and playfulness. The Bloodhound might also turn out to be too large for some families for whom a lethargic dog would otherwise be ideal. A further disadvantage of the Bloodhound might be its lowest-decile ranking on household protection.

Weight: 90 pounds
Height: 26 inches
Build: Strong
Coat: Short
Color: Black and tan,
   red and tan,
   or tawny

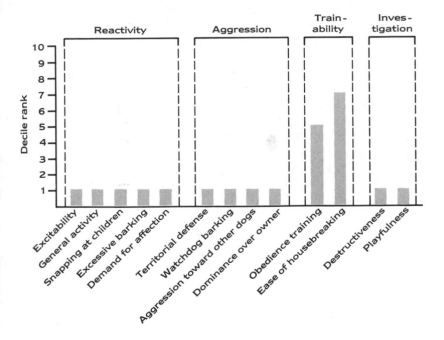

Boston Terrier

The Boston Terrier is a cross between the Bulldog and the English Terrier, but it is distinctive in its own right. Its conformation, which is also quite distinctive, strongly appeals to some people. On reactivity the Boston is similar to other terriers, but prospective owners may find that its higher rank on demand for affection—fifth from the top—makes it more attractive. To its credit as a possible family breed, the reactivity factor on which it ranks lowest is snapping at children. Note that the rank of seven is still a little high for families with young children, however.

On overall aggressive traits the Boston Terrier excels in watchdog barking, and it ranks only medium on its tendency to exert dominance over its owner. If property protection is a strong priority, you might look for a breed with a higher rank on territorial defense, but at least you can count on the Terrier's having a watchdog sound. Consider boosting the potential for territorial defense by choosing a male. With its medium rank on the trainability traits, the Boston Terrier rates higher than average for terriers as a whole.

Among alternative breeds, the tiny Maltese is unusual for its midrange ranking in aggressive traits and its receptivity to training similar to that of the Boston Terrier. Or you might nudge up each factor a bit by considering the Silky Terrier. If you can live with higher rankings on reactivity and aggressive traits, you can select from a large group of the smaller dogs that have great variety in coat color and conformation in other terrier breeds.

Weight: 19 pounds
Height: 14 inches
Build: Very light
Coat: Smooth, glossy
Color: Black with white

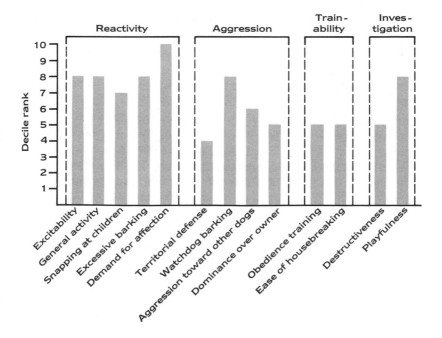

Boxer

If you're in the market for a good family dog but place a high priority on territorial protection, the Boxer might fill this role quite nicely. This is especially true if you're concerned about the high aggression rankings of guard dogs like Akitas, Dobermans, and Rottweilers but still want a dog that comes across as meaning business to intruders. The Boxer also ranks lower on destructiveness than the breeds that are typical of guard dogs.

The behavioral profile of the Boxer is moderate in all its traits—not too reactive (it has been used as a guide dog), not too sluggish, not terribly aggressive—but no pushover, either. With its average overall rank on obedience training, you should be able to shape the behavior of your Boxer to suit your lifestyle and needs.

Gender selection gives you the option of some flexibility on aggression and trainability. By choosing a female you can expect to enhance trainability, with some lessening of all the aggressive elements, including territorial guarding. By choosing a male you can expect stronger territorial defense but a greater tendency toward dominance and less enthusiasm for being trained. The Boxer's moderate level of playfulness is also fairly unusual for a breed with some watchdog capacity.

A slightly more reactive breed, with a comparable level of aggressive traits, but lower playfulness and a higher rank on obedience training, is the Welsh Corgi. You may like the lower tendency to exert dominance over the owner of this breed. The Corgi can be expected to challenge you less often for dominance and to glide more smoothly through obedience training than would a Boxer.

Weight: 70 pounds
Height: 23 inches
Build: Solid
Coat: Short, smooth
Color: Fawn or brindle
   with white

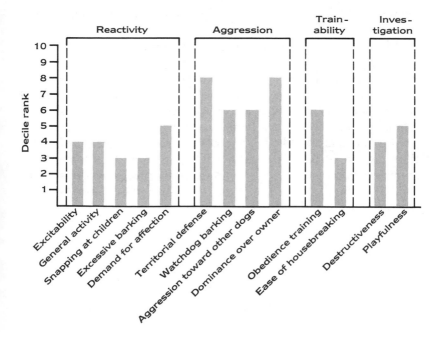

Brittany Spaniel

The Brittany Spaniel, along with spaniels in general, stands out for being very low in aggressive traits. This breed is within the lowest five on territorial defense, aggression toward other dogs, and the tendency to exert dominance over its owner. Furthermore, it ranks high on obedience training and low on snapping at children. Such a cluster of traits is often sought by families with small children or by adults who prefer not to have their dominance challenged by their dogs.

The Brittany Spaniel has a lower rating on reactivity traits than the Cocker Spaniel. The Brittany is also markedly lower on snapping at children and on its demand for affection. It also ranks lower than the Cocker on wanting to exert dominance over its owner but higher on obedience training. The English Springer Spaniel is more reactive than the Brittany, with a high rank on demand for affection and a very low one on snapping at children. The Springer, like the Brittany, ranks quite low on aggression, but it is stronger on watchdog barking, if that is one of your important priorities. The Springer's higher rankings on playfulness and destructiveness complement its generally higher reactivity compared with the calmer, quieter Brittany.

When compared with two other similar breeds that are often suggested for families, the Australian Shepherd and the Golden Retriever, it can be seen that the Brittany lacks their high rankings on demand for affection and playfulness. The Australian Shepherd or the Collie retain many characteristics of the Brittany's profile but rate higher on the two main traits relating to property protection: territorial defense and watchdog barking. As a possible drawback to choosing the Brittany, our authorities portrayed it as being much poorer on home protection than most other breeds. Another breed very like the Brittany, but higher on playfulness and lower on destructiveness, is the Vizsla.

Weight: 35 pounds
Height: 19 inches
Build: Light
Coat: Wavy
Color: White with orange

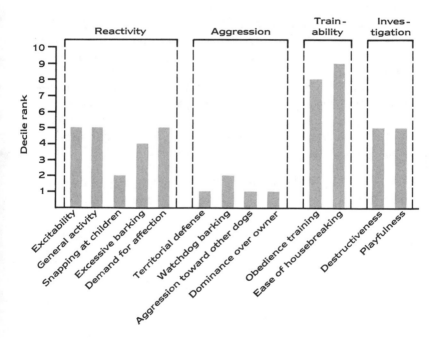

Bulldog

The Bulldog is well suited for the environment of the college fraternity, where it has enjoyed considerable success as a mascot. It ranks low on overall reactivity, not barking or snapping much, and not reacting much to noise and hubbub. The Bull channels its aggressiveness not into household protection—who needs a watchdog in a fraternity house?—but into survival: aggression toward other intruding mascots and resistance to domination by owners. It is just as well that no one expects a mascot to be obedience trained, for the Bulldog ranks among the lowest on this trait. Fortunately, it is slightly higher in ease of housebreaking. Assuming you're not on a fraternity's mascot-selection committee but love the Bull's unique face and conformation, you can expect to improve its suitability for normal homes by selecting a female.

The Bulldog has some traits that recommend it to certain households. Its rank in dominance over owner is only medium. The Bulldog's highest rank within reactivity—snapping at children—still is below average, and selecting a female would tend to mellow this trait. Finally, the Bulldog ranks third lowest of all breeds in general activity. If jittery, nervous dogs drive you crazy, you can feel secure in choosing a Bulldog, particularly since it also ranked second lowest of all the breeds on both destructiveness and playfulness.

As alternatives, the Norwegian Elkhound and the Old English Sheepdog both have more moderate overall ranks. The Sheepdog reaches the fourth decile on its highest factor, reactivity, and the Elkhound is characterized by moderate trainability traits.

Weight: 50 pounds
Height: 15 inches
Build: Sturdy
Coat: Short
Color: White and tan

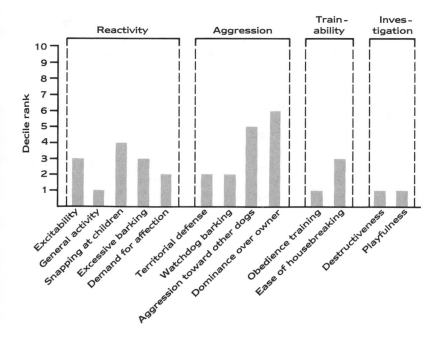

Cairn Terrier

Many terriers were bred to hunt, and though they are no longer used for hunting, the in-bred traits for hunting persist. The Cairn Terrier was trained to be effective at cornering otters and driving them from tiny hiding places. Cairns thus had to be active and aggressive and had to bark a lot. Note that the Cairn ranks quite high—fifth from the top—on excessive barking.

Otters are playful. Whether Cairns also had to be playful to hunt them effectively can't be determined, but the Cairn ranks fourth from the top in playfulness. Considering its breeding history and body size, this terrier has a relatively moderate behavioral profile. Some prospective dog owners may find the Cairn's high ranks on reactive and aggressive traits to be too strong, but several other terriers rank higher.

Particularly if you favor small terriers, you must expect them to have a lively profile. Small breeds are likely to rank high on reactivity, and most terriers (except the Yorkie) also rank high on aggression. The trainability of terriers ranges only from low to medium, excepting the larger higher-ranking Airedale. All things considered, the Cairn is one of the more moderate terriers, the Silky being another. If your preference is not necessarily for terriers but is for tiny dogs and you would prefer greater ease of training and lower aggression, further possibilities include the Shih Tzu, the Bichon Frise, or the Toy Poodle.

The colorful personalities of the small, lively breeds greatly endear them to their owners. They are good company for a person who lives alone. If you have a calm, consistent lifestyle and are usually at home, you may find a quieter, more docile version of the Cairn that is perfect for you. On balance, and according to the rankings, the Cairn is one of the most manageable of the terriers.

Weight: 14 pounds
Height: 10 inches
Build: Very light
Coat: Harsh, profuse,
  short; little shedding
Color: Wheat, tan, or
  grizzled

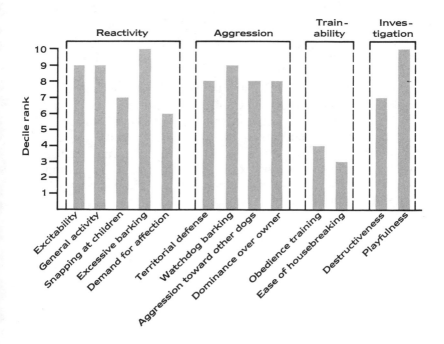

Chesapeake Bay Retriever

The Chesapeake Bay Retriever ranks low on overall reactivity and is considered among the most favored breeds for families with its rankings among the bottom few on excitability and barking. One gets the feeling that a concerted effort must have gone into breeding a dog with such low reactivity but as full of affection as the Chesapeake. The Chesapeake is a modest version of a watchdog and territorial defender, yet still is quite manageable in dominance contests with its owner. The aggression level of the Chesapeake has increased to a moderate level, and a high rank on obedience training complements this breeding.

The Chesapeake shares with two other retrievers, the Labrador and the Golden, high rankings on the trainability traits, manageable tendencies toward dominance, and an at least average rating on demand for affection. The Chesapeake is the only one of these three that's medium on aggressive traits (the others are low). The Golden Retriever's medium rank on reactivity exceeds that of both the Lab and the Chesapeake, but the Chesapeake exceeds the Golden in its rank on home protection. The other breed with a profile most like that of the Chesapeake is the Collie. The Collie would be a good no-nonsense choice for someone wishing a watchdog, because of its low rankings on dominance over owner, destructiveness, and demand for affection, and its moderate levels of territorial defense and watchdog barking. The Australian Shepherd also shows moderate promise as a watchdog, particularly if you prefer somewhat higher reactivity than shown by the Chesapeake.

Weight: 70 pounds
Height: 24 inches
Build: Solid
Coat: Dense
Color: Brown or tan

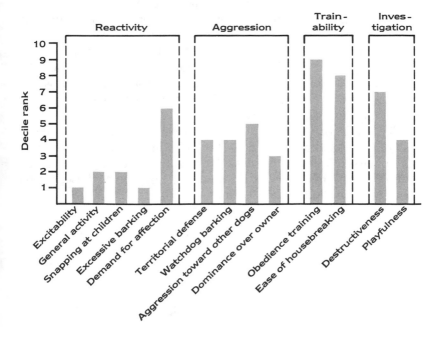

Chihuahua

If you're looking for the most lively, feisty dog per pound of body weight, the Chihuahua is probably it. The Chihuahua is the very smallest of all breeds and ranks fifth from the top on general activity, as well as extremely high overall on reactivity traits.

You might find it best to warn visiting children that your Chihuahua really is a dog, not a toy—and a rather peppery one at that—despite its small size. The Chihuahua's high rank on snapping at children seems to bear out the prevailing notion that they aren't good with children. At least with this dog's small size, snapping will not inflict real damage to larger children. The Chihuahua's profile includes a high rank not only on snapping at children but also on excessive barking. Although these two traits can be nuisances, they may not emerge if your lifestyle is especially calm and consistent.

On overall aggression the Chihuahua ranks high, and its high level on attempting to exert dominance over its owner could be troublesome. If you are sold on Chihuahuas, consider selecting a female to soften the dominance characteristic. Finally, the Chihuahua's low rankings on destructiveness and playfulness are unusual among tiny dogs. It might take better to being left alone during the day than would some other breeds.

The West Highland White Terrier has a breed profile similar to that of the Chihuahua, except that the Westie has high levels of both playfulness and destructiveness. If you'd like a less aggressive version of the Chihuahua that is still a tiny dog, the Maltese is a bit more trainable and may be such a possibility.

Weight: 4 pounds
Height: 5 inches
Build: Fragile
Coat: Short or long; cold
 sensitive
Color: Various

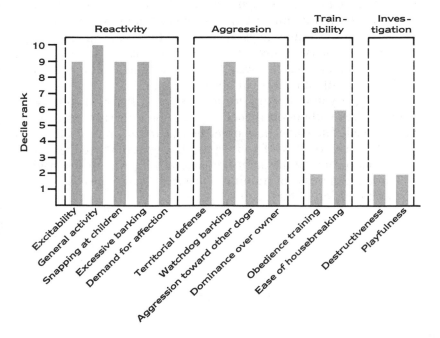

Chow Chow

Devotees of the Chow Chow appear to be drawn to this breed's unique conformation and the one-man loyalty reputedly typical of it. The Chow is the breed highest ranked on territorial protection, for those concerned about home protection. Perhaps its lowest ranking of all breeds on obedience training is related to the respected reputation the Chow has for being somewhat unpredictable in aggressiveness.

Our respondents assigned extreme rankings to the Chow on most traits and seldom used medium ratings. The Chow is not only the highest-ranked breed on territorial defense but is also second in its tendency to exert dominance over its owner and third in exhibiting aggression toward other dogs. It is ranked third in snapping at children but is otherwise low in reactivity and is the lowest-ranked breed for demanding affection. And as mentioned, it is the lowest-ranked breed of all for ease of obedience training.

Clearly, if you're looking for a cuddly dog that will romp with your children without obedience training, the Chow is not an appropriate breed. The Chow does excel as a guard dog, but it is likely to be a challenge to train. If you want a less extreme breed, examine the similar profile of the Saint Bernard, with its slightly less aggression and greater ease of training. The Great Dane's profile shows a further extension of these traits.

Weight: 60 pounds
Height: 20 inches
Build: Sturdy
Coat: Profuse, long;
 regular grooming
 desirable; heavy
 shedding at times
Color: Red or black

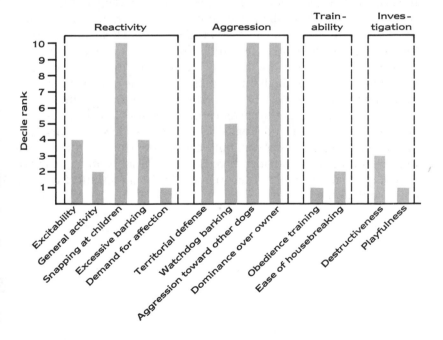

Cocker Spaniel

The Cocker Spaniel ranks very near the top on its demand for affection, right behind the Toy and Miniature Poodles, which may be the main reason the Cocker is among the most frequently registered breeds. Aside from its craving for affection, which is the only trait where the Cocker approaches an extreme ranking, it ranks medium on other reactivity characteristics.

Although the Cocker has long been a popular family pet, it does not excel in the traits often favored by people wanting a family pet: high obedience training and playfulness, and low dominance over owner and snapping at children. More family-style ratings on these traits can be found in the retrievers and poodles, breeds that also have very high rankings on demand for affection. The Cocker ranks solidly in the middle on the trainability traits, destructiveness, and playfulness.

The four spaniels profiled in the book—the Brittany, the Cocker, the English Springer, and the tiny subcompact model, the Maltese—reflect more disparity than that in other conventional groups like the terriers, hounds, and retrievers. Each spaniel ranks especially low on aggression, relative to similar dogs. In fact, what all spaniels have in common is a low level of aggression, though they range from medium to very high on obedience training and from medium to high on reactivity. Note, however, that some trainers and breeders have mentioned the occurrence of atypical or excessive aggression in some Cocker and English Springer Spaniels. The Brittany and English Springer Spaniels both exceed the Cocker in the rankings on trainability. Smaller breeds are invariably more reactive than larger ones, so it is not surprising that the tiny Maltese is more reactive than the Cocker.

Weight: 25 pounds
Height: 14 inches
Build: Light
Coat: Wavy, soft, long;
  regular grooming
  customary
Color: Black, red, buff

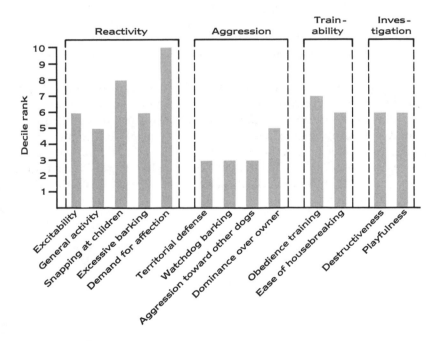

Collie

To some people the Collie is almost unique in having a profile often favored for family pets but a level of aggression that makes it about average as a watchdog for home protection. The Collie has a number of attractive behavioral traits. It is moderately ranked on territorial defense and watchdog barking, yet manages to rank low on the sometimes troublesome traits of aggression toward other dogs and dominance over its owner.

The Collie's scoring on a number of other traits should also help make it easy to live with. It ranks high on obedience training and housebreaking, average on playfulness, and extremely low on both destructiveness and snapping at children. The only other thing you might ask for in a family pet would be a higher ranking on its demand for affection. Although the Collie is quite trainable, it won't be attending to you and your movements at every minute of the day.

Another breed that has similar possibilities as a watchdog but still ranks low on aggression toward other dogs and exerting dominance over its owner is the Australian Shepherd. This breed is quite unlike the Collie in its higher scores on general activity and demand for affection. The Chesapeake Bay Retriever ranks moderate on aggressive traits but it lacks the finely balanced higher aggressive factor on home defense and lower emphasis on aggression toward other dogs and family members that the Collie has.

Weight: 65 pounds
Height: 24 inches
Build: Solid
Coat: Long, dense,
  straight; regular
  grooming desirable;
  heavy seasonal
  shedding
Color: Sable and white, or
  in combination with
  either gray or black or
  gray and black

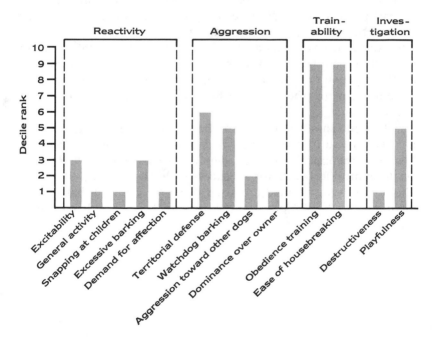

Dachshund

Much of the popularity of the Dachshund probably relates to its moderate level of reactivity, which is most unusual in tiny dogs, coupled with its being a spirited playmate and a believable watchdog. Many people also find the shape of the Dachshund appealing and are often surprised to find that its conformation comes in a variety of sizes, right down to tiny.

The Dachshund ranks consistently about average on reactivity traits. Our authorities were asked to rate the common Dachshund, so there might be reason to think that as the size gets smaller the reactivity level will go up. Note the slope of the four characteristics for aggression on the accompanying graph, which shows a pattern comfortable for owners. That is, it ranges from high on territorial defense down to moderately high on dominance over owner. In short, the Dachshund will serve you as a watchdog but may contest you for dominance to some extent.

The Dachshund ranks average on playfulness, but the positive side of its characteristics seems to end here. The Dachsie is the second lowest of all breeds on ease of housebreaking and ranks high on destructiveness. If you're an aspiring Dachsie owner, take comfort in the reminder that these two traits are the least reliably predicted ones and that environment plays an important role in the development of them both. As a warning, though, the Dachsie ranks low on the trainability traits. It could be a challenge. Consider selecting a female to boost the potential for ease of obedience training and housebreaking.

Two other smallish breeds, the Beagle and the Pug, are similar to the Dachshund in overall reactivity and ease of training. Both are low in aggression, though, and won't serve as watchdogs. Remember to avoid the Beagle for its excessive barking, if you like quiet. Should you prefer a medium-sized dog, you will find that several, including the Welsh Corgi and the Airedale Terrier, rank in the middle on reactivity.

Weight: 20 pounds
Height: 9 inches
Build: Light
Coat: Short
Color: Various

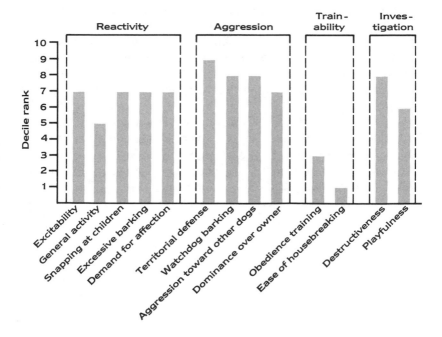

Dalmatian

The Dalamatian is certainly one of the most interesting-looking breeds, with such a distinguished-sounding name that it was used in the successful movie title "101 Dalmatians." And who can imagine any breed but the Dalmatian as a fire engine mascot? With such high visibility for the breed it may come as a surprise that the Dalmatian has a rather middle-of-the-road profile.

None of the positive or negative aspects of this profile rate a strong warning, but many of the subtleties of the Dalmatian's rankings happen not to be those customarily preferred. For example, the Dalmatian ranks medium on reactivity traits but high on snapping at children and low on demand for affection. Similarly, though it ranks in the middle on overall aggressive traits, the profile is high on aggression toward other dogs and for dominance over owner. The Dalmatian's very high rank on destructiveness and fourth-lowest rank of all breeds on ease of housebreaking might make it less troublesome in a firehouse than in a home. Keep in mind, however, that these traits are the least reliably predicted of all. And the Dalmatian's moderate ranking on obedience training might encourage you to try shaping specific traits in the direction you prefer. Also, you can expect the Dalmatian to make a good contribution toward home protection.

Only one other breed, the Weimaraner, is similarly moderate on both reactivity and aggression. However, the Dalmatian has a slight edge in aggression, and the Weimaraner is a bit higher in reactivity. These are subtle differences, though, and are probably not significant. The Boxer also tends to be moderately reactive, but it excels over the Dalmatian on territorial protection.

Weight: 45 pounds
Height: 21 inches
Build: Solid
Coat: Short, sleek; regular
grooming desirable;
heavy shedding
Color: Black spots
on white

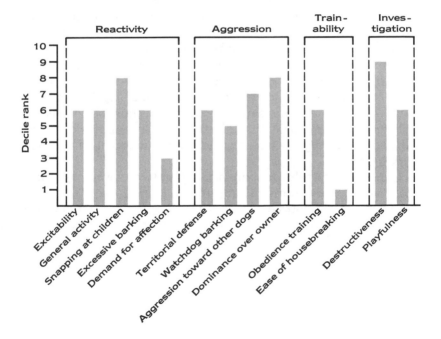

Doberman Pinscher

The Doberman Pinscher is the epitome of the guard dog and disciplined protector. It is top ranked on ease of housebreaking and is second from the top on obedience training. The Doberman also ranks among the top few breeds on territorial defense and watchdog barking, two traits critical for territorial protection.

The profile of the Doberman can best be seen against the background of similar profiles like those of the German Shepherd, the Rottweiler, and the Akita. The Shepherd's profile corresponds remarkably well except that the Shepherd ranks very high on destructiveness and high on playfulness, whereas the Doberman is only about average on these two traits. Other subtle differences from the Shepherd are the Doberman's lower rankings on excitability and excessive barking, higher rating on demand for affection, and higher rank on obedience training. The Akita and Rottweiler differ in that they display very low reactivity and playfulness.

If you're considering a guard dog that will also be a family pet, the four breeds just mentioned may be more aggressive and powerful, and less easily dominated, than you would like. Even with a moderate ranking on exerting dominance over their owners, these breeds require from the owner and family a willingness to discipline the dog whenever there is a confrontation over dominance.

Some other breeds are less highly tuned as guard dogs but still have the good watchdog trait of being highly trainable and having high rankings on territorial defense and watchdog barking. The Welsh Corgi and the Standard Poodle are two trainable breeds with only modest ranks on dominance over owner and aggression toward other dogs but high rankings on territorial defense and watchdog barking.

Choosing a female Doberman is certainly one way of reducing the tendency of this breed to be aggressive toward other dogs. Given the Dobie's high scores on watchdog barking and territorial protection, a female can be expected to excel in home protection.

Weight: 70 pounds
Height: 27 inches
Build: Solid
Coat: Short, smooth;
 little shedding
Color: Black, red, blue

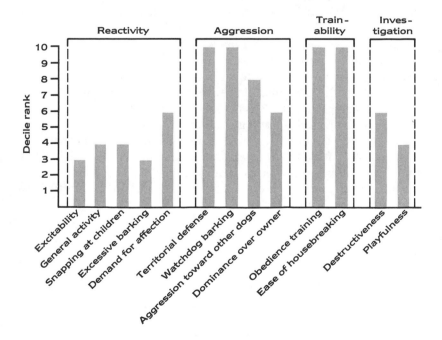

English Springer Spaniel

The English Springer Spaniel vies with the Cocker for being the most popular spaniel. These two breeds share an extremely high ranking on demand for affection, which may account for their reputations as loving, devoted dogs. As a family pet, the Springer would be a safer bet, because of its lower ranking than the Cocker on snapping at children and dominance over owner.

Like the Brittany Spaniel, the English Springer Spaniel ranks low in overall aggression, but it has a higher score on watchdog barking than either the Brit or the Cocker, if you're looking for household protection. The Springer's reactivity, like the Cocker's, is high. The Springer is the second most playful of all breeds and ranks very high on obedience training. With these rankings it has much of what people want most in a family pet, particularly if they're looking for a fairly lively breed. However, the Springer's above-average level of destructiveness is a trait you may want to note with caution.

If you'd love a tiny dog and can live with a smaller dog's higher reactivity, remember that there's a toy spaniel, the Maltese (discussed later). But the small dog with a profile most closely resembling the Springer's is the Bichon Frise, described earlier. Watch out for its higher level of snapping at children, though.

If you are seriously interested in this breed, investigate its reported idiopathic or abnormal aggressive behavior, which takes the form of unwanted vicious attacks on people. This characteristic would appear to be a genetic aberration that could be spotted by reviewing a dog's ancestry.

Weight: 50 pounds
Height: 20 inches
Build: Average
Coat: Long, smooth;
   regular grooming
   customary
Color: Combinations of
   white with liver or
   black, possible tan
   markings

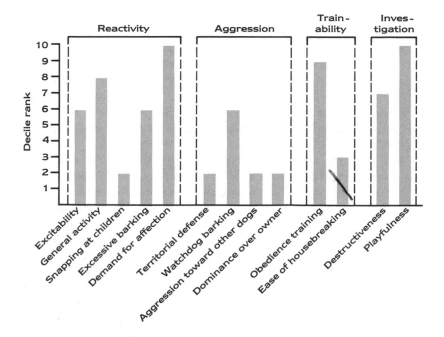

Fox Terrier

The Fox Terrier was bred to harass foxes out of good hiding places by focusing all its attention, growls, and barks on this task. The Fox Terrier's profile seems ideally suited for chasing foxes but much less appropriate if you want a polite, attentive, obedient dog.

When a breed ranks in the extreme on eight of the thirteen key behavioral traits, this bears noticing. The Fox Terrier was ranked by our respondents as being the most excitable breed of all, the second highest on excessive barking, and the third highest on general activity. This overall reactivity is undoubtedly useful for steady persistence during a fox hunt. With its very high overall ranking on aggression, the Fox Terrier is the second-highest breed on aggression toward other dogs and is very high in its exertion of dominance over its owner.

If you want a lively dog for your home, the Fox Terrier breed may be one to consider. However, you can expect this breed to require some obedience training. You may well find training to be a challenge, since the Fox Terrier ranks among the lowest three breeds on obedience training and ease of housebreaking and is the third highest in destructiveness. If you have a small apartment with no yard, you might consider whether you're prepared to cope with a possible destructiveness problem, and if so, how. Of course, avoiding the problem may be the best solution. But the Fox Terrier is a small dog, so its impact on your lifestyle through its high rankings on reactivity, aggression, and destructiveness would be much less than if it were a larger breed. And as with other breeds, by selecting a female you can reduce the impact of aggressive traits and boost the dog's trainability.

If you decide that a Fox Terrier is livelier than you need but you still want a small dog, the tiny Silky Terrier described later has more favorable rankings on exerting dominance over its owner, obedience training, and destructiveness. Selecting a larger dog like the Airedale Terrier would of course eliminate the extremely high rating on reactivity. The Airedale's rankings on ease of training and dominance over owner are also more suitable for most owners. Finally, consider the Cairn Terrier, which has fewer extremely high ranks than the Fox Terrier and seems slightly more moderate across the board, except for its excessive barking, a holdover from its old otter-hunting days.

Weight: 17 pounds
Height: 15 inches
Build: Very light
Coat: Hard, wiry, or
   smooth; regular
   grooming customary
Color: White with black
   or tan

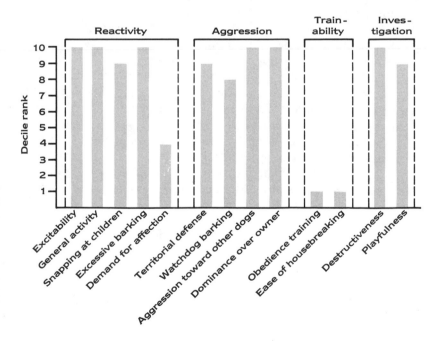

German Shepherd Dog

The German Shepherd Dog is the classic guard dog, which may explain its high popularity. The Shepherd's reputation is consistent with its rankings of 10 on watchdog barking and territorial defense. The Shepherd stands apart from other breeds that are also ranked high on watchdog barking and territorial guarding by being rated higher on overall reactivity and destructiveness.

The Shepherd is not for the fainthearted who back away at a small growl or dislike meting out discipline. Its guard-dog behavior is linked to high overall aggression, particularly toward other dogs, and a high tendency to resist domination by its owner. Given the Shepherd's rating near the top on ease of obedience training, the dog–owner relationship is likely to thrive most if the Shepherd is given systematic obedience training.

Because of the high popularity of this breed and the variety of roles it fills in guarding, guiding the blind, and as a family pet, you should expect considerable variability from one dog in this breed to another. It is definitely worth exploring the genetic line of a Shepherd you may be considering.

If the Shepherd's spirit appeals to you but you'd like to soften its aggressive and destructive tendencies, consider selecting a female. And if the Shepherd's high destructiveness really concerns you, two other guarding breeds, the Akita and the Rottweiler, rank very low on this trait.

Weight: 75 pounds
Height: 25 inches
Build: Sturdy
Coat: Dense; regular
grooming desirable
Color: Browns, black,
and tan

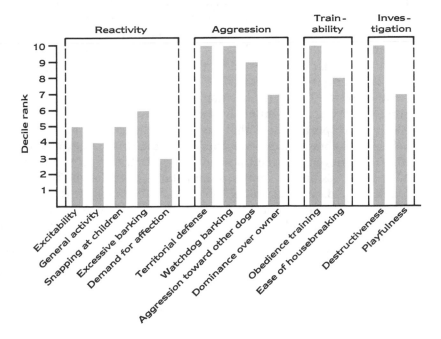

German Shorthaired Pointer

The streamlined looks of the German Shorthaired Pointer emphasize the fine tuning that went into developing it as an outstanding breed for field performance. Nevertheless, the rather moderate-ranking profile of this breed suggests that it might easily fit into a number of different lifestyles. If you examine the behavioral profiles of the various sporting breeds, you'll see that they invariably rank higher than average on ease of training, especially obedience training. But you may be disappointed if you're expecting this in the German Shorthaired, because it ranks only medium and rates lowest of all the field-sporting breeds. Thus, with a German Shorthaired Pointer even as a pet you shouldn't expect the same responsiveness in taking it through obedience classes as you would from a Golden Retriever or Labrador Retriever. Another possible problem with this breed is that you may be expecting a breed with moderate behavior, but its high rank on destructiveness may prove frustrating.

To its credit as a possible family member, the German Shorthaired Pointer ranks below average on snapping at children and is a solid medium on its demand for affection. This pointer will be attentive but won't follow you around every minute of the day. By selecting a female you might edge up its rankings on obedience training and ease of housebreaking and reduce its level of general activity and destructiveness.

Although the German Shorthaired Pointer is the only pointer profiled in this study, you might want to consider a number of the other classic sporting dogs that are within the same general type, such as the Labrador Retriever, the Vizsla, the Brittany Spaniel, the Golden Retriever, and the Chesapeake Bay Retriever. If you'd like to boost aggression and ease of training but reduce destructiveness, a Collie would be a possibility to consider. The Golden Retriever and the Vizsla are two breeds with lower aggression, and the Australian Shepherd, Collie, Labrador Retriever, and Golden Retriever rank higher on ease of training.

Weight: 60 pounds
Height: 24 inches
Build: Average
Coat: Short
Color: Liver or
liver with white

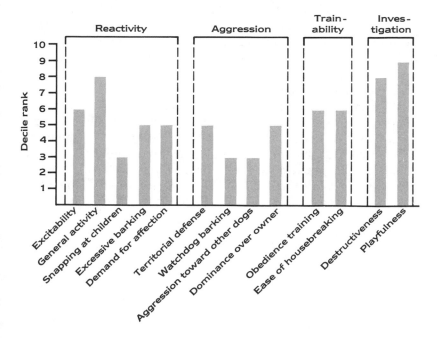

Golden Retriever

The profile of the Golden Retriever may justify for you its reputation as a very good family pet. The Golden ranks the lowest of all breeds on snapping at children and the second lowest on excessive barking. Its reportedly high level of demand for affection of course adds to its appeal as a children's pet. And it was the bottom-ranked breed both on aggression toward other dogs and on dominance over owner, so it is not likely to stir up trouble with people or other dogs. Its lack of aggressive challenge is enhanced all the more by its high ranking on obedience training. Finally, the Golden displays another family-favorite combination—low destructiveness paired with high playfulness, despite low activity and excitability.

One drawback of the Golden for many people is its low ranking on territorial defense and watchdog barking. Its combination of ease of training and low aggression, though not appropriate for a guard dog, could work well in some institutional settings with children. But its playfulness would most likely be a drawback for the elderly or for severely ill or handicapped people.

It's a challenge to suggest other breeds that might be close to the Golden's particular combination of rankings. Perhaps the Vizsla most closely matches the Golden's overall profile. You should get acquainted with this breed, if you'd like a more unusual dog. The Australian Shepherd also shares many of the Golden's traits. It offers more promise than the Golden as a territorial defender and watchdog, because of its somewhat higher rating on aggression.

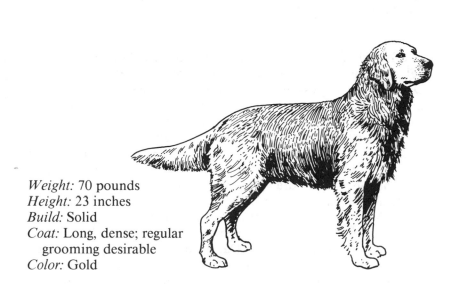

Weight: 70 pounds
Height: 23 inches
Build: Solid
Coat: Long, dense; regular
 grooming desirable
Color: Gold

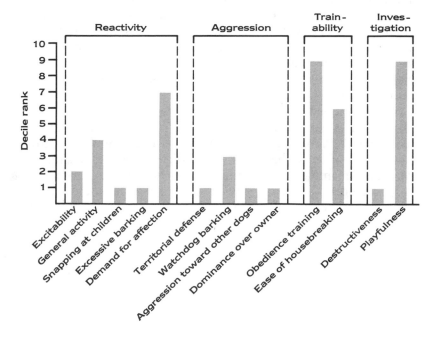

Great Dane

The huge Great Dane, with its ninth-decile ranking on territorial defense, has few equals for home protection. Fortunately, the Dane's other aggression-related traits are tempered somewhat so that with appropriate discipline its average ranking on the tendency to exert dominance over its owner should make it a manageable pet.

As you might expect in such a large breed, historically bred as a guard dog, the Great Dane consistently ranks low on general reactivity, resulting in a very low overall score. Greatly in its favor is that the Great Dane differs from most similar dogs in ranking as moderately receptive to obedience training.

Anyone contemplating getting an extremely large dog would be wise to examine not only its specific behavioral traits but also the implications of body size. The Dane ranks only average on destructiveness, so this factor is normally not a major concern with it. But an only moderately destructive dog weighing 150 pounds can obviously create damage far beyond what the top-rated Fox Terrier can match, even given plenty of time to do the job. And aggression by a huge dog can create an array of problems different from the nips of a small, snappy dog. Furthermore, caring for a Dane or any other notably large dog with the potential for aggression or destruction requires a significant commitment from its owner to be responsible for requiring acceptable behavior from the dog. Anyone unable to make such a commitment should consider other breeds that are less demanding in this respect.

As one alternative, the Saint Bernard has a profile much like the Dane's, but it has lower rankings on destructiveness and watchdog barking and is a bit higher on dominance. If you prefer the strong, silent spirit of the Dane—but want a slightly smaller version—the Alaskan Malamute has a similar profile, though it is very high on destructiveness. A version half the size of the Dane, the Boxer, is slightly more reactive than the Dane but is otherwise quite similar to it.

Weight: 130 pounds
Height: 32 inches
Build: Very strong
Coat: Smooth
Color: Brindle, fawn

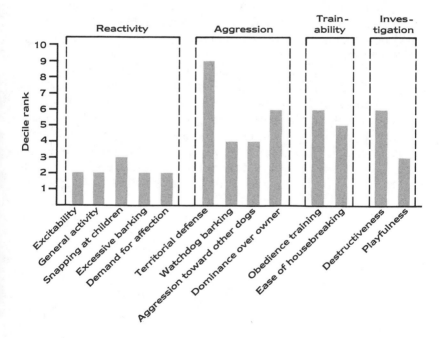

Irish Setter

The Irish Setter, ranked the most playful of all breeds, is a playmate that is always ready for action. It is also within the top few breeds on general activity, being far livelier than most other dogs of its size. High reactivity is usually found in smaller breeds, but compared with similar dogs like the terriers and spaniels the Setter is reportedly lower on aggression and is more receptive to training. Many people find attractive the Setter's rusty color and coat fringed with long hair, called feathers, as well as its exuberant spirit. And for all its high reactivity and playfulness, the Setter ranks low on snapping at children. Do note, however, that it ranks high on destructiveness.

If you favor the Setter's general profile but are interested in a breed high on ease of training, look into the English Springer Spaniel, described earlier. If you need more than the Setter's low aggression, the Boston Terrier ranks medium on these traits and high on watchdog barking. Our authorities ranked the Setter and the Boston Terrier as being similar in reactivity, ease of training, and playfulness. Finally, if you're captivated by the playfulness of the Setter but can't abide even moderate destructiveness, use these two traits to compare the Golden Retriever, the Standard Poodle, the Shetland Sheepdog, and the Vizsla.

Keeshond

Weight: 65 pounds
Height: 26 inches
Build: Average
Coat: Long, "feathery";
regular grooming
desirable
Color: Mahogany

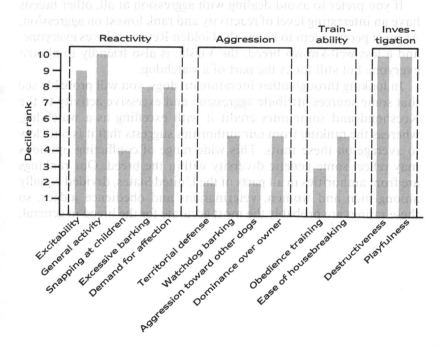

Keeshond

The Keeshond is another of the sled-dog look-alikes that is mild mannered, easy to train, and active enough to be a noticeable part of family life, according to our authorities. Its behavioral profile reflects reactivity and aggression traits close to average but low general activity, snapping at children, territorial defense, dominance over owner, and destructiveness. The Keeshond thus appears to be an easily managed dog that is compatible with a family setting.

From the Keeshond's profile it is difficult to predict any inevitable problems. Dogs in general serve as effective watchdogs for most people, so a medium ranking on this trait is probably sufficient for guarding and detecting intruders. You can, of course, get the maximum potential for territorial defense by choosing a male. You might also take advantage of the Keeshond's strongest rank, obedience training, to have a well-mannered dog and to enhance its territorial protection, or to tone down its medium ranking on excessive barking, if you like quiet.

If you prefer to avoid dealing with aggression at all, other breeds have an interesting level of reactivity and rank lowest on aggression. As most people seem to know, the Golden Retriever loves everyone, and a less well-known breed, the Vizsla, is also friendly to almost everyone but still looks the part of a watchdog.

In looking through other literature on dogs, you will probably see that some sources attribute aggression and excessive activity to the Keeshond and sometimes credit it with excelling as a watchdog, whereas the ranking from our authorities suggests that it is only low to average on these traits. This wide range of conflicting opinions may reflect some genetic diversity within the breed. Our rankings are from authorities in all parts of the United States, divided equally among men and women, veterinarians and obedience judges, so these ratings are probably the most accurate for the breed in general.

Weight: 40 pounds
Height: 18 inches
Build: Average
Coat: Profuse, thick;
    odorless; regular
    grooming desirable;
    seasonal shedding
Color: Grays

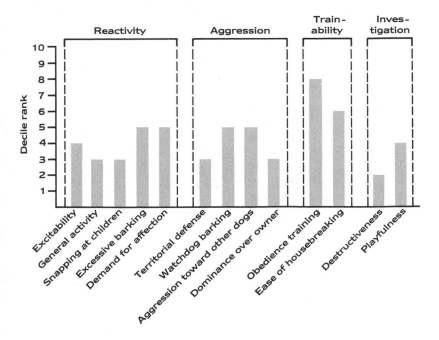

Labrador Retriever

The Labrador Retriever is the prototypical family-type breed with moderately low reactivity and aggression but a high ranking on obedience training. This breed is one of the classic examples of a breed's being outstanding in field work but nevertheless having the qualities that make it an ideal family dog.

In keeping with its reputation as a good dog for children, the Lab ranked the second lowest of all breeds in snapping at children, its only extreme ranking. Its remaining ranks on reactivity are low, except for its medium ranking on demand for affection. What this means is that the Lab will pay attention to children and seek affection even though in other respects it has a relatively unreactive temperament.

In aggression the Lab ranks slightly higher on territorial protection than on aggression toward other dogs and people. You might want to boost this breed's potential for territorial defense by selecting a male. This agreeable combination of aggressive traits is further supported by the Lab's high rankings on training and housebreaking. Finally, although the Lab ranks high in playfulness, it ranks low in destructiveness.

The Lab ranks as moderate among similar retrievers and shepherds. If you prefer the least aggressive breeds of this general type, try the Vizsla or the Golden Retriever. For a stronger watchdog the Collie is a possibility. The Australian Shepherd was rated the most easily trainable dog of this sort. Our authorities ranked both the Chesapeake Bay Retriever and the Newfoundland as being lower than the Lab on excitability.

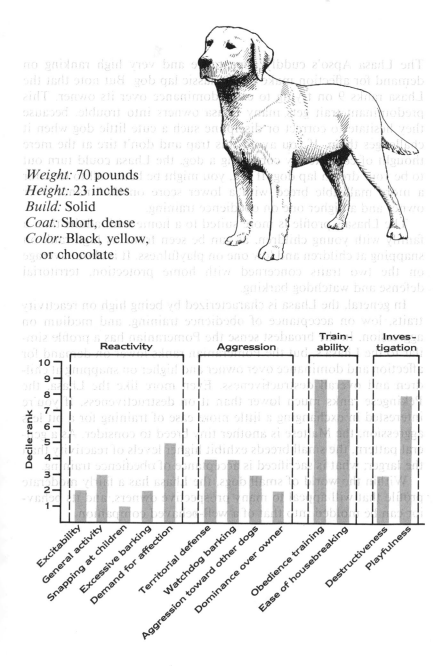

Weight: 70 pounds
Height: 23 inches
Build: Solid
Coat: Short, dense
Color: Black, yellow,
  or chocolate

Reactivity | Aggression | Train-ability | Inves-tigation

Decile rank — 1 to 10

Excitability · General activity · Snapping at children · Excessive barking · Demand for affection · Territorial defense · Watchdog barking · Aggression toward other dogs · Dominance over owner · Obedience training · Ease of housebreaking · Destructiveness · Playfulness

Lhasa Apso

The Lhasa Apso's cuddly appearance and very high ranking on demand for affection make it the classic lap dog. But note that the Lhasa ranks 9 on trying to exert dominance over its owner. This predominant trait gets many Lhasa owners into trouble, because they hesitate to correct or discipline such a cute little dog when it challenges them. If you avoid this trap and don't tire at the mere thought of consistently correcting a dog, the Lhasa could turn out to be your dream lap dog. If not, you might be better off to look for a more malleable breed with a lower score on dominance over owner and a higher one on obedience training.

The Lhasa's profile is more suited to a home with adults than a family with young children, as can be seen from its high rank on snapping at children and low one on playfulness. It is about average on the two traits concerned with home protection, territorial defense and watchdog barking.

In general, the Lhasa is characterized by being high on reactivity traits, low on acceptance of obedience training, and medium on aggression. In the broadest sense the Pomeranian has a profile similar to the Lhasa's, but the Pomeranian ranks lower on demand for affection and dominance over owner and higher on snapping at children and overall destructiveness. Even more like the Lhasa, the Pekingese ranks much lower than it on destructiveness. If you're interested in exchanging a little more ease of training for a bit less aggression, the Maltese is another tiny breed to consider. As a general pattern, the small breeds exhibit higher levels of reactivity than the larger; what is sacrificed is acceptance of obedience training.

Within the world of small dogs, the Lhasa has a fairly moderate profile that will appeal to many prospective owners, and its behavior can be molded into that of a well-behaved companion.

Weight: 15 pounds
Height: 10 inches
Build: Very light
Coat: Profuse, long;
  regular grooming
  customary
Color: Gold, black, gray,
  or white

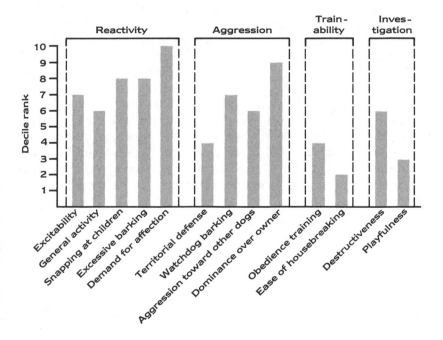

Maltese

Many people are drawn to the smallest breeds either because they want a manageable dog or because they just want a dog that's minimally demanding of food, space, and care. But to find a small dog that doesn't rank high on reactivity or aggression or low on ease of training takes some searching. The Maltese is a tiny dog that ranks moderate on trainability traits and fairly low on aggressive traits. Perhaps because it is a toy spaniel, the Maltese has this profile combination that is so rare in little dogs.

The Maltese, which is quite moderate in behavior, has no extreme rankings. As do almost all the very small breeds, the Maltese ranks high overall on reactivity, but its level of general activity is only medium. And though it ranks low on overall aggression, its rank on watchdog barking is a strong medium. The low destructiveness of the Maltese also recommends it.

Of course, any time you find a breed that can slide into your grocery bag on top of the milk and eggs, the dog's size is its most evident characteristic. Particularly because of its ranking on obedience training and its manageable level of aggression, you may find children thinking that the Maltese is really a cat that would love to ride in a doll carriage. This could be a costly mistake, because the Maltese ranks high on snapping at children.

A logical breed to consider if you like the Maltese's profile is another spaniel, the Cocker. As you might expect, the primary difference in these two breeds is that the larger Cocker Spaniel is lower on reactivity. The Shih Tzu is another breed with a profile similar on reactivity and aggression, but it ranks higher in the trainability area.

Weight: 6 pounds
Height: 6 inches
Build: Frail
Coat: Long, silky, flowing;
   little shedding with
   regular grooming
Color: White

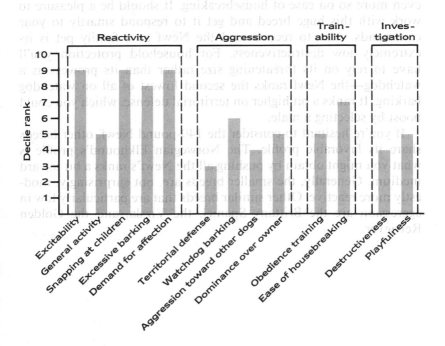

	Reactivity	Aggression	Trainability	Investigation

Decile rank

Reactivity: Excitability 9, General activity 5, Snapping at children 9, Excessive barking 8, Demand for affection 9

Aggression: Territorial defense 3, Watchdog barking 6, Aggression toward other dogs 4, Dominance over owner 5

Trainability: Obedience training 5, Ease of housebreaking 7

Investigation: Destructiveness 4, Playfulness 5

Newfoundland

Some people are attracted to the idea of having a huge dog that looks like it could be quite a threat but is a cream puff inside. If you're one of these, you'll probably find that the Newfoundland comes closer to this idea than any other large breed. No other breed combines the Newfoundland's low reactivity and aggression with such a high ranking on training. Both the Great Dane and the Saint Bernard, for example, rank much higher on aggression.

The Newfoundland is a quiet dog. Where it does rank high is in just those traits that contribute to its compatibility as a family pet. Its rank on demand for affection is a warm 6, though it otherwise ranks as one of the lowest four breeds on all the other reactivity traits. Because the Newfoundland's rank on demand for affection is so much higher than on these other traits, this characteristic has probably been specifically selected for in breeding the Newf. A high demand for affection was seen as a desirable trait for the Newf in its historic role of guarding and rescuing children.

Note that the Newfoundland is strong on obedience training but even more so on ease of housebreaking. It should be a pleasure to work with this huge breed and get it to respond smartly to your commands. Also to recommend the Newf as a family pet is its extremely low destructiveness. For household protection you'll have to rely on its threatening size rather than its prowess as a watchdog—the Newf ranks the second lowest of all on watchdog barking. It ranks a bit higher on territorial defense, which you could boost by selecting a male.

If you're hesitant to consider the 140-pound Newf, other breeds share its favorable profile. The Norwegian Elkhound's profile is what you might obtain by pushing all the Newf's ranks a bit toward medium. Generally, the smaller breeds are, not surprisingly, modestly more reactive. Other similar breeds that are particularly low in aggression are the Brittany Spaniel, the Vizsla, and the Golden Retriever.

Weight: 140 pounds
Height: 28 inches
Build: Massive
Coat: Dense, undercoat; regular grooming desirable; heavy seasonal shedding
Color: Black, white and black

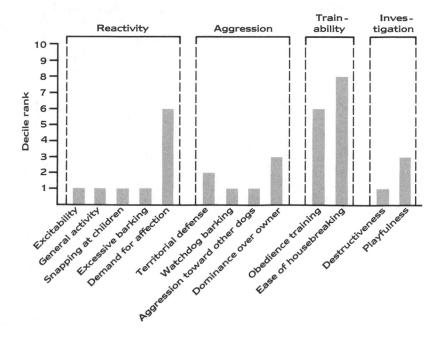

Norwegian Elkhound

The Norwegian Elkhound was bred to hunt elk during Arctic winters, so it is not surprising that its appearance strongly resembles that of the nothern sled dogs. However, unlike the sled dogs or their look-alike the Akita, which excel in one or another form of aggression, what you get in the Norwegian Elkhound is the low rankings in aggressive traits that are more characteristic of the hounds. And along with its low to moderate aggression, the Elkhound ranks in the bottom decile on watchdog barking and is only medium on territorial defense.

Despite these low rankings on aggression, it is not unusual to see references to the Elkhound as a guard dog or watchdog. Although it is true that almost all breeds can serve to a degree as watchdogs, the Elkhound did not stand out in this respect in the rankings of our authorities. Whatever its behavior, the Elkhound doesn't look like a dog anyone would want to tangle with, which may serve as a deterrent. The Elkhound may simply look the part of a watchdog enough to serve that role.

The Norwegian Elkhound ranks fairly low on reactivity and aggression. If you're not familiar with the behavior of this breed, it falls into the same general group as the more well-known Bloodhound. Relative to similar breeds, the Elkhound has a low level of excitability, general activity, snapping at children, excessive barking, and demand for affection, all the traits within low reactivity. To its credit as a nice household pet for the right family, the Elkhound ranks in the low to moderate range on destructiveness and is medium on playfulness.

If you'd like to nudge up the reactivity traits slightly, for an alternative breed consider the Boxer. And if a high ranking on trainability is a priority, try the Labrador Retriever, which otherwise rates about the same as the Elkhound on reactivity and aggression.

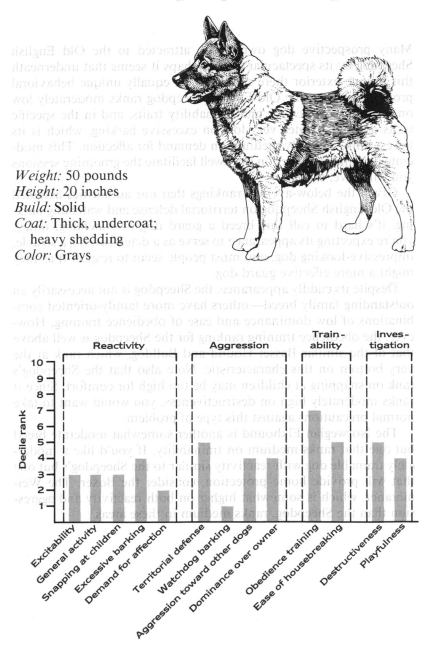

Weight: 50 pounds
Height: 20 inches
Build: Solid
Coat: Thick, undercoat;
  heavy shedding
Color: Grays

Old English Sheepdog

Many prospective dog owners are attracted to the Old English Sheepdog by its spectacular coat. Perhaps it seems that underneath this unique exterior there should be an equally unique behavioral profile. However, the Old English Sheepdog ranks moderately low on reactivity, aggressive and trainability traits, and in the specific traits as well. It rates very low on excessive barking, which is its lowest rank, and only medium on demand for affection. This moderate demand for affection may well facilitate the grooming sessions you will have, though.

Given the below-average rankings that our authorities assigned the Old English Sheepdog on territorial defense and watchdog barking, it's hard to call this breed a guard dog or watchdog, unless you're expecting its appearance to serve as a deterrent. It's a sizable, impressive-looking dog, and most people seem to respect it as they might a more effective guard dog.

Despite its cuddly appearance, the Sheepdog is not necessarily an outstanding family breed—others have more family-oriented combinations of low dominance and ease of obedience training. However, the obedience training ranking for the Sheepdog is well above that of the similar Basset Hound and Bulldog, which rank at the very bottom on this characteristic. Note also that the Sheepdog's rank on snapping at children may be too high for comfort. Since it ranks moderately high on destructiveness, you would want to take normal precautions against this type of problem.

The Norwegian Elkhound is another somewhat moderate breed but one that ranks medium on trainability. If you'd like a moderately trainable dog with reactivity similar to the Sheepdog's but one that will provide home protection, consider the Boxer. The Weimaraner, which is somewhat higher on both reactivity and aggression than the Sheepdog, ranks medium in these areas.

Weight: 95 pounds
Height: 24 inches
Build: Strong
Coat: Long, profuse;
   extensive grooming
   required; little shedding
Color: Bluish and white

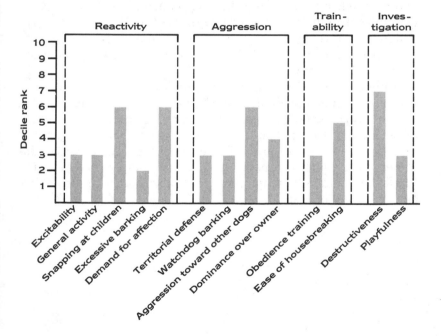

Pekingese

In many respects the Pekingese—small, highly reactive, and demanding of affection—is a classic lap dog. If you've already examined the profiles of other small or toy breeds, you'll have seen that high reactivity carries with it high ranks on excitability, snapping at children, and barking, along with strong demand for affection. Most small breeds rank high on aggression, whether toward other dogs or that involved in resisting dominance by the owner. If you want a lap dog and are prepared to cope with these traits, which characterize the Peke, it may be for you.

Notice that the Pekingese ranks low on the trainability traits, and it is fourth from the bottom in ease of housebreaking. However, the extra attention needed in this area may be balanced for you by the Peke's third-lowest rank out of all breeds on destructiveness. But ease of housebreaking and destructiveness are the least predictive traits, so don't let these rankings be the main determining force in your selection of a breed. Both traits are quite amenable to training and favorable influence from the environment. Finally, the Pekingese ranks medium on the watchdog traits of barking and territorial defense, but it is high on aggression toward other dogs and in dominance over its owner. The Peke is thus not for the owner who wants a pet that's a pushover.

Among the small breeds having somewhat similar profiles, the Boston Terrier and the Maltese are higher ranked in trainability, but they are still good on home protection by virtue of their high ratings on watchdog barking. These two breeds lack the Peke's high rankings on aggression toward other dogs and dominance over the owner and are higher in both playfulness and destructiveness. The Lhasa Apso and Pomeranian, which are also similar to the Pekingese, are higher in destructiveness.

Weight: 9 pounds
Height: 6 inches
Build: Very light
Coat: Long, profuse;
      annual shedding
Color: White with tan,
      fawn, red, black

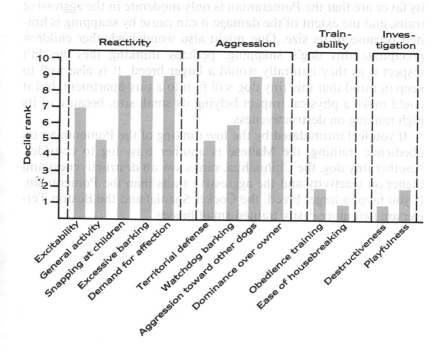

Pomeranian

The Pomeranian's overall profile is one of high reactivity, low trainability, and medium aggression. It is one of the tiniest dogs, and generally the smaller the breed, the higher the level of reactivity. To be rated at only the eighth decile in excitability is relatively modest for a five-pound dog, and some Pomeranians are in fact very calm.

We must point out that the Pomeranian received the top ranking on snapping at children. Its low rating on obedience training and high ranking on destructiveness are further causes for concern. In its favor are that the Pomeranian is only moderate in the aggressive traits, and the extent of the damage it can cause by snapping is limited because of its size. One might also wonder whether children precipitate this dog's snapping, perhaps thinking they needn't respect it as they naturally would a larger breed. It is also well to keep in mind that this tiny dog will fit into a tiny apartment, but it could make a physical impact belying its small size, because of its high ranking on destructiveness.

If you feel intimidated by the low ranking of the Pomeranian on obedience training, the Maltese is another tiny dog to consider. Another tiny dog, the Chihuahua, ranks low on destructiveness and higher on reactivity and the aggressive traits than the Pomeranian. If you favor a larger breed, the Cocker Spaniel and the Boston Terrier are two more easily trained small breeds.

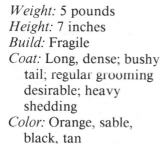

Weight: 5 pounds
Height: 7 inches
Build: Fragile
Coat: Long, dense; bushy
 tail; regular grooming
 desirable; heavy
 shedding
Color: Orange, sable,
 black, tan

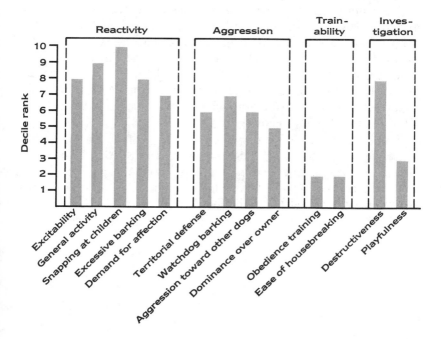

Poodle (Miniature)

The poodles in general rank as some of the breeds most frequently registered with the AKC, and the Miniature Poodle is the most sought after of all poodles. If you'd like a dog that's active and alert but would give you disciplined and obedient attention, consider the popular Miniature Poodle.

Ranked the highest of all breeds on its demand for affection, the Miniature is also considered within the top few breeds on obedience training and ease of housebreaking. The common lore about poodles emphasizes what is often referred to as their high intelligence. The intelligence that is often attributed by people to poodles may simply be the way they ideally represent a combination of behavioral characteristics: high demand for affection, an excellent rank on obedience training, a high level of reactivity, and low dominance over the owner.

It is interesting to examine the profiles of all three poodle breeds: the Miniature, the Standard, and the Toy. Notice first that in dogs with smaller bodies the rankings on reactivity traits increase. The small differences between the Miniature and the Toy on obedience training, destructiveness, playfulness, and territorial defense are probably of only minor significance. Thus, for poodles, body size and reactivity provide a sliding scale useful to use in balancing your ideals to match your needs.

Some other breeds with roughly similar profiles are the Bichon Frise, the English Springer Spaniel, and the Shetland Sheepdog. Some prospective dog owners who may want the poodle's profile but with a lower level of reactivity might consider the Golden Retriever or the Australian Shepherd.

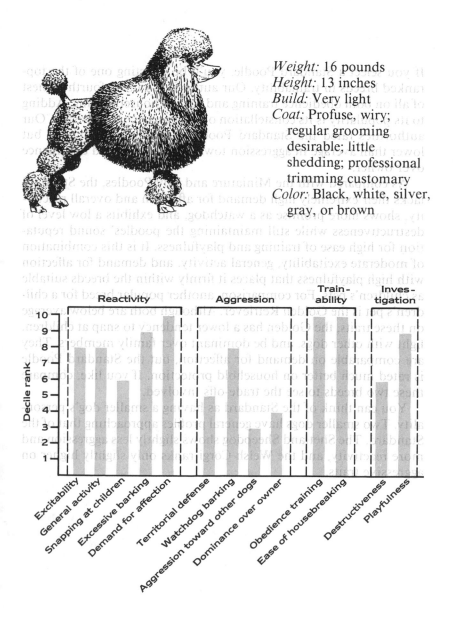

Poodle (Standard)

If you select a Standard Poodle, you'll be selecting one of the top-ranked breeds in trainability. Our authorities rank it fourth highest of all on both obedience training and ease of housebreaking. Adding to its popularity is its constellation of aggressive characteristics. Our authorities rated the Standard Poodle a promising watchdog but lower than average in aggression toward other dogs and dominance over owner.

As compared with the Miniature and Toy Poodles, the Standard lacks their extremely high demand for affection and overall reactivity, shows more promise as a watchdog, and exhibits a low level of destructiveness while still maintaining the poodles' sound reputation for high ease of training and playfulness. It is this combination of moderate excitability, general activity, and demand for affection with high playfulness that places it firmly within the breeds suitable as children's pets. For comparison, another popular breed for a children's pet is the Golden Retriever. Although both are below average on these traits, the Golden has a lower tendency to snap at children, fight with other dogs, and be dominant over family members. They are comparable on demand for affection, but the Standard Poodle is rated much better on household protection. If you like, compare these two breeds to see the trade-offs involved.

You can think of the Standard as having a smaller dog's personality. Two smaller dogs have general profiles approaching that of the Standard. The Shetland Sheepdog shows slightly less aggression and more reactivity, and the Welsh Corgi ranks only slightly higher on aggressive traits.

Weight: 55 pounds
Height: 23 inches
Build: Average
Coat: Wiry, close curls; regular grooming desirable; professional trimming customary; little shedding
Color: Black, white, silver, gray, or brown

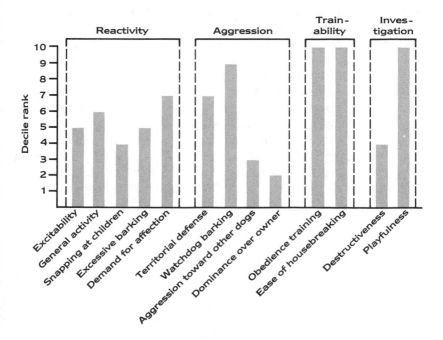

Poodle (Toy)

Not surprisingly, the Toy Poodle's profile closely resembles that of the Miniature Poodle, and the differences, though small, may influence your choice of a puppy. Both breeds rank high on reactivity. On demand for affection the Toy ranks second, just below the Miniature. Although it is still high on obedience training, the Toy falls two deciles below its breed mates the Standard and the Miniature, which is probably what causes some people to rate the Toy below them in intelligence. (Some of the elements that people seem to associate with intelligence in dogs are the tendency of these dogs to pay attention to you all the time and a high level of excitability and general activity.)

The Toy Poodle would appear not to be as good a choice for a family pet as the Miniature or the Standard, because of its higher rankings on snapping at children and exerting dominance over its owner, plus being lower in playfulness. And though you could do worse on home protection, keep in mind that the Toy ranks below the Miniature in both watchdog barking and territorial defense.

As with most small dogs, the tiny Toy Poodle's spirit seems to have expanded to compensate for its diminutive size, if you associate spirit with general reactivity. Of course, for many owners the Toy Poodle's size is its primary attraction. If your highest priority is to have a tiny dog, two other similar breeds have personalities resembling the Toy Poodle's. The Shih Tzu, which ranks only medium on snapping at children and excessive barking, otherwise closely parallels the Toy. And the Bichon Frise, not as close a match, may interest you if you aren't looking for a watchdog.

Weight: 6 pounds
Height: 9 inches
Build: Frail
Coat: Heavy, curly;
 regular grooming
 desirable; little
 shedding; professional
 trimming customary
Color: Black, white, silver,
 gray, or brown

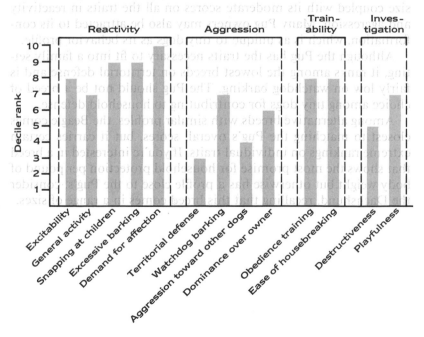

Pug

As one of the toy breeds, the Pug is quite unusual in being moderate on overall reactivity and low on aggression. To see how distinct this breed is from similar breeds, take a look at such profiles of tiny breeds as the Silky Terrier, the Yorkshire Terrier, the Toy Poodle, and the Chihuahua.

If you're looking for a relatively quiet, nonreactive breed, many others surpass the Pug and are lower on aggressive traits, but these are all larger breeds. The remarkable thing about the Pug is its small size coupled with its moderate scores on all the traits in reactivity and aggression. Many Pug owners may also be attracted to its conformation, which is as unique to tiny dogs as its behavior profile.

Although the Pug has the traits necessary to fit into a family setting, it ranks among the lowest breeds on territorial defense and is fairly low on watchdog barking. The Pug should not be a breed of choice among tiny dogs for contributing to household defense.

Among alternative breeds with similar profiles, the Beagle comes closest to matching the Pug's overall scores, but it carries certain extreme rankings on individual traits. If you're interested in a breed that shows the most promise for household protection per pound of body weight but otherwise has a profile close to the Pug's, consider the Dachshund, recalling that this breed comes in a range of sizes.

Weight: 16 pounds
Height: 10 inches
Build: Very light
Coat: Short, smooth
Color: Fawn, dark face

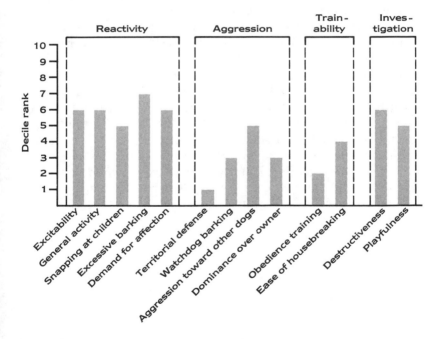

Rottweiler

The Rottweiler is one of the largest of the more highly respected guard dogs, the others being the Akita, the Doberman Pinscher, and the German Shepherd Dog. Ranking in the top decile for the aggressive traits, the Rottweiler is among the top few breeds in territorial defense and watchdog barking. Unlike the Doberman and the Shepherd, though, it has a low ranking on general reactivity. In particular, this breed is among the lowest on excitability, excessive barking, and demand for affection. As a further contrast with the Shepherd, the Rottweiler has a low ranking on destructiveness and playfulness. Its profile is on the whole most like that of the Akita.

Because guard dogs are traditionally associated with four breeds, you can easily study the individual differences in their profiles before making your selection. The Rottweiler ranks at the extremes of lower or higher deciles on five traits, whereas the other three breeds are at one or the other extreme on four traits. The Rottweiler's two very high ranks, on territorial defense and watchdog barkings, are those most relevant to territorial protection. The highly trainable nature of the Rottweiler makes it quite deserving of its reputation as a splendid guard dog.

If we use the frequency of breeds' registration as a measure of their popularity, the Doberman and the Shepherd rate among the most popular, with the Rottweiler and the Akita being less common. We can only wonder whether their extremely low rankings on reactivity—including demand for affection—and playfulness account for their lesser popularity. If you're sold on Rottweilers but need a territorial defender and want some integration of the dog into the family, consider getting a female to boost demand for affection and perhaps make dominating the dog somewhat easier.

Weight: 110 pounds
Height: 25 inches
Build: Very strong
Coat: Short, undercoat; weekly brushing desirable
Color: Black with rust

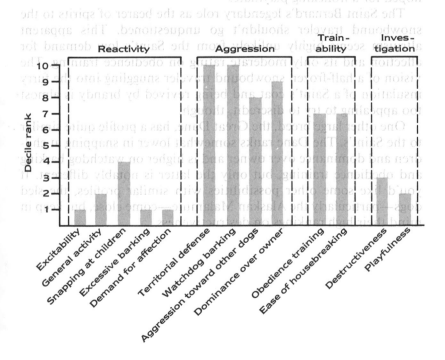

Saint Bernard

What of course bowls you over at first about the Saint Bernard is its sheer size. As if by necessity, this breed's impact is somewhat balanced by its very low general reactivity. The Saint in fact follows the general rule that the larger the breed the lower the reactivity.

Except for its very low rank on watchdog barking, the Saint is rated high on the aggressive traits, particularly on territorial defense and the tendency to exert dominance over its owner. You can expect to have some dominance confrontations, but you can rely on good home protection from this breed. Certainly its size and high rank on territorial defense make an impressive combination.

If you can appreciate the challenge of giving obedience training to a dog that may be bigger than you are, you might consider the Saint Bernard, which ranks low to moderate on obedience training. Given its size, the Saint's low rank on destructiveness is welcome. Its extremely low playfulness may be a concern, however, if you'd hoped for a frolicking playmate.

The Saint Bernard's legendary role as the bearer of spirits to the snowbound traveler shouldn't go unquestioned. This apparent altruism seems highly unlikely from the Saint's low demand for affection and its only moderate rating on obedience training. The vision of a half-frozen snowbound traveler snuggling into the furry insulation of a Saint's coat and being revived by brandy is almost too appealing to try to discredit, though.

One other large breed, the Great Dane, has a profile quite similar to the Saint's. The Dane ranks somewhat lower in snapping at children and dominance over owner and is higher on watchdog barking and obedience training, but only the latter is notably different. If you'd like some other possibilities with similar profiles, the sled dogs—particularly the Alaskan Malamute—come close, but keep in mind their high rankings on destructiveness.

Weight: 165 pounds
Height: 28 inches
Build: Massive
Coat: Long or short,
  dense; heavy shedding
Color: White with red or
  brindle

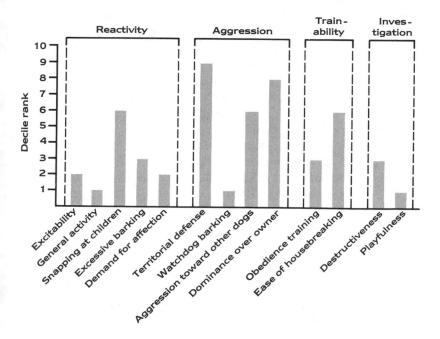

Samoyed

The Samoyed is in the group of sled dogs with the Alaskan Malamute and the Siberian Husky that manifest low reactivity, high aggression, and low trainability. All three breeds also rank below average in demand for affection and playfulness, and they rank high in destructiveness. All three are stronger than average on territorial guarding, but the Samoyed ranks higher than the others on watchdog barking; the Malamute and the Husky rank in only the second decile on this trait. Perhaps the Samoyed's watchdog barking, the most pronounced of all the sled dogs, relates to its historical background in guarding reindeer.

For anyone concerned with the tendency of sled dogs to exert dominance over the owner, the Samoyed, ranking at the seventh decile on this trait, is a better choice than the Husky, which is at the ninth decile. However, given the sturdy build of the Samoyed, its low ranking on obedience training, and its high destructiveness, this breed is best suited to an owner willing to provide systematic obedience training.

Having an outdoor run available for the Samoyed may help avoid the problem of destructiveness. On the other hand, this breed's low reactivity suggests that it might tolerate even a small apartment for at least part of the day. The breeding background of this and the other sled dogs was in the snowy north, of course, and they do prefer the rugged outdoors. Any dog, or person, for that matter, can be more fit with some outdoor exercise. In particular, for the Samoyed and the other sled dogs it seems that dog companionship ranks higher in importance than human contact. The Samoyed's low rank on demand for affection and high level of aggression toward other dogs are consistent with the idea that it is predisposed to pay more attention to dogs than to people.

If you prefer a sled dog with less reactivity, especially the excessive barking, you might consider the Alaskan Malamute, which ranks low on this trait. Interestingly, both the Malamute and the Husky are strong on territorial defense but low on watchdog barking. In comparing the Samoyed to the Husky, you'll find the Husky very high on aggression toward other dogs, dominance over the owner, and destructiveness. As with all the sled dogs, selecting a female may reduce the strength of the aggressive traits and increase the acceptance of obedience training.

Weight: 55 pounds
Height: 22 inches
Build: Solid
Coat: Thick; regular
   grooming desirable,
   heavy annual shedding;
   virtually odorless
   when dry
Color: White

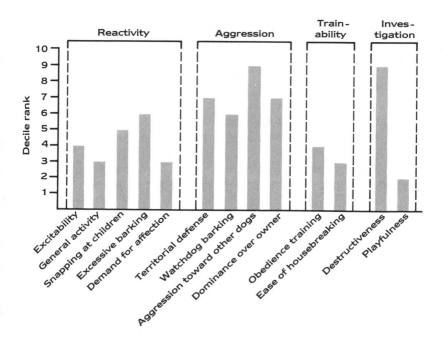

Schnauzer (Miniature)

The Miniature Schnauzer is among the most popular breeds in terms of its frequency of AKC registration. Its appeal is undoubtedly its cute face, smallish size, and liveliness, as indicated by its high rankings on excitability and general activity. The Miniature Schnauzer is distinguished by ranking on the extremes of several scales. Our authorities rated this breed within the top five on nine of the thirteen key behavioral traits, but the Schnauzer ranked among the top few breeds on each of the aggressive traits and was the top breed of all on both watchdog barking and aggression toward other dogs. On reactivity the Schnauzer was ranked within the top few breeds for each trait except demand for affection. It was ranked third from the top on playfulness. You'll probably always know when there's a Schnauzer around.

The Schnauzer falls midrange on obedience training and is high on destructiveness. From the Schnauzer's profile, it is easy to understand that this terrier was bred in Germany to be successful at catching rats. We cannot in good conscience recommend the Miniature Schnauzer as a family or children's pet. Yet the fact that it has successfully served in this capacity is testimony to the importance of the early obedience training and behavioral shaping that can help mold a dog's adult behavior.

Another spirited terrier, the most similar to the Schnauzer, is the West Highland White Terrier. Of the two breeds the Schnauzer is the more trainable and playful, and the less destructive. For those who appreciate the toy breed, the Silky Terrier is less aggressive than the Schnauzer, is less destructive, and, of course, is significantly smaller.

Weight: 15 pounds
Height: 13 inches
Build: Very light
Coat: Wiry; little
   shedding; regular
   grooming desirable
Color: Black, salt and
   pepper

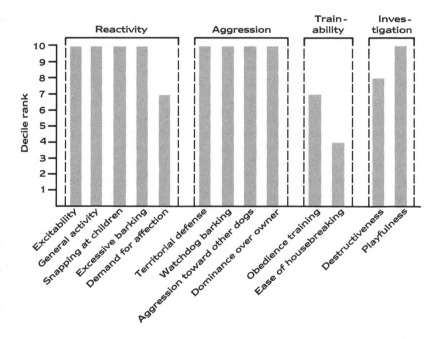

Scottish Terrier

It's easy to see how the Scottish Terrier has so many devotees, from its pert appearance and spunky personality. The Scottie is one of the distinguished terriers, ranking in the top deciles on five reactivity and aggressive traits. Despite ranking high on excitability and snapping at children, it is somewhat low in demand for affection and is only moderately high on general activity and excessive barking. The Scottie's overall rank on reactivity is thus moderate for a tiny terrier.

The Scottie is top dog for exerting dominance over its owner, a rating which suggests that it may have fully earned its reputation as an independent spirit. This is not a dog for people who want mild-mannered obedience or who are unwilling to be assertive. Fortunately, the Scottie is small, so it has less potential for causing injury or damage than would a larger dog with the same ranking. And though the Scottie doesn't star in obedience training, it is far from being the lowest-ranked breed, so making a consistent effort at obedience training is likely to be fruitful.

With its high potential for snapping, the Scottie is certainly not a breed for children. Nor do its apparently high potential for destructiveness, its above-average rank on excessive barking, and its extreme rank on aggression toward other dogs recommend it as a prototypical family dog. You can expect the Scottie to make outstanding attempts at property protection, but its small size is a liability. And with its high aggression toward other dogs, one wonders if the famous Black and White Scotch whiskey logo had to be drawn rather than photographed when it was discovered that the Scottie couldn't be photographed that close to another dog.

You may love terriers but be intimidated by now by this profile of Scotties. If so, the Silky Terrier and Cairn Terrier rank as less aggressive and destructive and more trainable than the Scottie. The Yorkshire Terrier ranks as moderate in aggression, but it is still high on watchdog barking, if that is a priority for you.

Weight: 20 pounds
Height: 10 inches
Build: Light
Coat: Thick, wiry; little shedding; regular grooming desirable, professional clipping customary
Color: Black or brindle

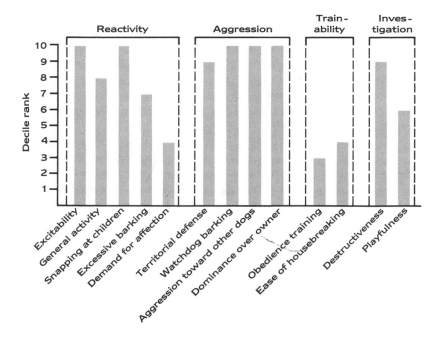

Shetland Sheepdog

The Shetland Sheepdog has all the characteristics we associate with a well-mannered, loving canine companion. Ranked third from the top in obedience training and third from the bottom in dominance over owner, and with high ranks on demand for affection, playfulness, and easy housebreaking, the Sheltie almost sets the standard for what a well-mannered, easily trained dog can be.

The breed with a profile most similar to the Sheltie's is the Australian Shepherd. Look at the Aussie's profile to see what the Sheltie also has to offer and where you might have cautionary concerns. Both breeds are similar in being outstanding in obedience training, extremely low on the tendency to be dominant, and high on the demand for affection. Not surprisingly, both breeds are beautiful performers in sheepdog trials. It is no wonder that Shelties are regulars in obedience classes. The Sheltie combines these traits with a stronger potential for home protection than the Aussie—what aggressive tendencies the Sheltie has are channeled into home protection—but it is somewhat more reactive, especially in snapping at children and excessive barking.

According to our authorities, excessive barking is not a trait that can be suppressed by selecting a certain sex, but snapping at children will likely occur a little less with a female. The Sheltie would obviously make a fine family pet, especially if it is introduced into a family when the children are old enough not to provoke snapping. Older children may enjoy training the Sheltie, and its playfulness should make its interaction with children rewarding for all concerned.

The Sheltie is smaller than the Australian Shepherd. If you want a still smaller dog, the Shih Tzu's profile is remarkably like the Sheltie's, without its extremes. For instance, the Shih Tzu remains low on dominance over owner, but it comes up to the fourth decile on this trait. The Standard and Miniature Poodles share with the Sheltie similar scores on aggression and high rankings on obedience training, playfulness, and demand for affection.

Weight: 16 pounds
Height: 14 inches
Build: Very light
Coat: Long, heavy; heavy
  seasonal shedding
Color: Black and sable
  with white or tan or
  white and tan

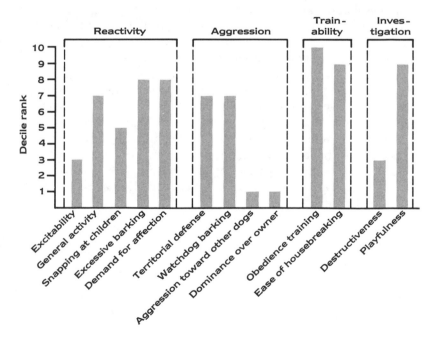

Shih Tzu

The name Shih Tzu, which means little lion in Chinese, must refer to this breed's performance as a strong watchdog rather than its overall aggression, because it ranks below average on the various aggressive traits. Both its name and its bark are bigger than its bite. In fact, the remarkable thing about this tiny breed is that although its reactivity is inevitably high, the two most objectionable related traits—snapping at children and excessive barking—are only average. Also to its credit, the Shih Tzu ranks fairly high on trainability. The little lion's profile comes about as close to replicating that of the Shetland Sheepdog as does any other small breed's.

Many tiny breeds rank high on snapping at children, excessive barking, dominance over owner, and destructiveness. Perhaps the most attractive feature of the small Shih Tzu is that it rates no higher than midrange on these four traits that sometimes prove troublesome. When compared with other tiny dogs, the Shih Tzu appears to be relatively manageable.

The Toy Poodle is a nudge higher than the Shih Tzu on overall reactivity and aggression. The tiny Bichon Frise is a less aggressive version of the Shih Tzu.

Weight: 12 pounds
Height: 9 inches
Build: Very light
Coat: Long, thick; regular
　grooming desirable
Color: Various

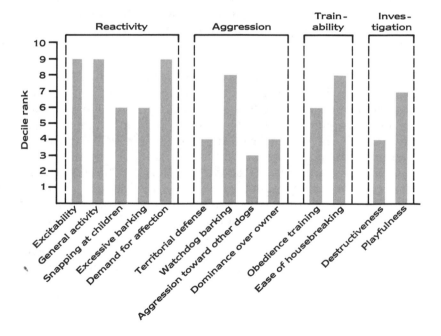

Siberian Husky

The Siberian Husky represents to most people the epitome of a rugged, hard-working, no-nonsense breed. Its behavioral profile of low reactivity, lack of enthusiasm for obedience training, and below-average demand for affection are consistent with this reputation.

The Husky ranks in the top few breeds on the tendency to exert dominance over its owner and on aggression toward other dogs. If you're willing to stand up to a sturdy dog's confrontations without backing down, the Husky, or another sled dog such as the Alaskan Malamute or Samoyed, may be the dog for you. But if you shy away from a dog's first growl at a small toddler or yourself, you'd do better with a breed scoring lower on dominance over owner.

Those who are impressed by the Husky's qualities of ruggedness may be surprised to learn that it ranks as the second highest of all breeds on general destructiveness. Although destructiveness is not the most predictable trait, this ranking is worth noting, particularly if you live in a small apartment and no outdoor dog run is available.

If you select a Husky, it is likely to serve you well for household protection, despite its low ranking on watchdog barking. Our authorities tended to imply that the Husky and the Malamute both show little hesitancy in attacking strangers and waste little time barking, which is consistent with their image of silent, reserved strength.

None of the sled dogs are very playful, but the Husky ranks in the fourth decile, the highest of the sled dogs. None of these breeds demand much affection, either, so before choosing a Husky be sure you don't dream of a dog that wants only to be attentive to you all day long. This breed may be more predisposed to paying most of its attention to other dogs.

If the Husky's moderate reactivity and high territorial protection appeal to you but you want a smaller dog, this could be a problem. All the breeds with modest reactivity are large dogs. If you must have a smaller dog, the best choice might be the Dachshund or the Welsh Corgi. The Dachshund shares the high aggression of the Husky, comes in a range of sizes, and ranks in the eighth decile on destructiveness. The Corgi is a more easily trainable and less destructive version of the Dachshund.

Weight: 50 pounds
Height: 22 inches
Build: Average
Coat: Thick; heavy
   shedding
Color: Varied, face
   markings

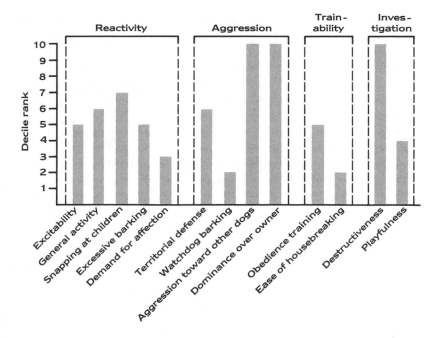

Silky Terrier

If you'd like a tiny dog that's moderately trainable, the Silky Terrier may be ideal. Although it is considered a toy, its profile is typical of the terriers, with a high rank on reactivity and a ranking among the top few breeds on excitability and general activity. However, its aggression level is only modestly high, and it ranks a strong medium on obedience training.

The Silky's respectably moderate scores on the tendency to exert dominance over its owner and on obedience training, coupled with its small size that makes aggressive transgressions manageable, suggest that the Silky may just pass as a family pet. It's necessary to watch out for small children, though, since the Silky is high on snapping at children. And keep in mind that its tendency toward excessive barking can make it a nuisance.

The Silky is characterized by being high on aggressive traits and medium on trainability traits. The Yorkshire Terrier, also a toy, closely corresponds to the Silky on reactivity and aggressive traits. The Boston Terrier, ranked evenly across the board for all behavioral traits, is probably a closer fit, though it is a larger dog.

Weight: 9 pounds
Height: 9 inches
Build: Fragile
Coat: Silky, glossy, long;
   little shedding
Color: Blue with tan

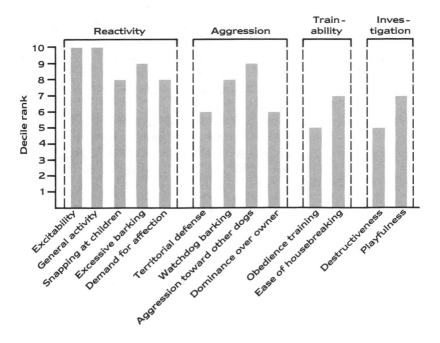

Vizsla

Maybe you'd like a dog that's completely harmless—but looks as if it would do some damage to an intruder. Unless you already know the Vizsla well, you may not recognize that it looks impressive as a territorial defender or watchdog, but can't be counted on to perform as well as other ones, according to our authorities. Perhaps the most remarkable thing about the Vizsla's profile is its low overall aggression. It ranks fifth lowest on watchdog barking. Clearly, you should be able to expect minimal problems with the Vizsla in terms of aggression toward other dogs and toward people in dominance contests. This breed, an unlikely looking hunting dog, was actually bred for pointing and retrieving upland game birds and waterfowl in Hungary.

In addition to its low rankings on aggressive traits, the Vizsla is high on a number of traits that families look for in a dog. It ranks as highly receptive to training and is moderately reactive, with a low rank on snapping at children. The Vizsla happily combines high playfulness with low destructiveness. The reason it hasn't caught on as a family breed may be that its sleek conformation and short hair don't suggest the cuddly children's playmate as well as the more popular family dogs do.

The Vizsla is rated among the trainable, unaggressive, calm dogs often favored by families. Compare its profile with the Golden Retriever's similar one. An Australian Shepherd, Chesapeake Bay Retriever, or Collie can probably be expected to perform as a watchdog as well as the Vizsla, but not to rank so high on dominance as to provide a major challenge.

Weight: 65 pounds
Height: 23 inches
Build: Average
Coat: Short, smooth
Color: Rusty gold

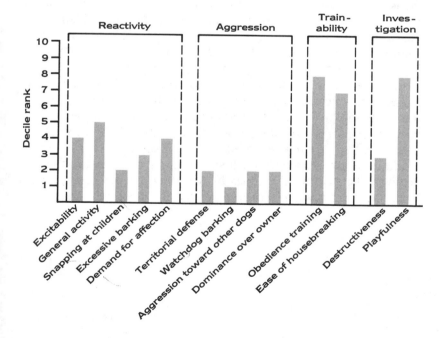

Weimaraner

One way to sort out the many rankings on behavioral characteristics is to consider a breed that's moderate in practically all its characteristics, such as the Weimaraner. With only one exception, it ranks between the third and seventh deciles on all traits.

The Weimaraner's moderate profile is unique for a dog its size. Its profile is usually found in a smaller dog, but the Weimaraner may be more suitable for romping through the countryside with you than would a Maltese or a Pomeranian. Other similarly profiled dogs are some of the small breeds and the Irish Setter.

The one exception in the Weimaraner's otherwise moderate profile is its high rank on destructiveness. Simply preventing opportunities for destructiveness may be the solution to this problem. Also, because destructiveness is one of the least well predicted traits, environment can make a considerable difference in this behavior.

As compared with the only other similar moderate-sized dog, the Irish Setter, the Weimaraner is less reactive, less playful, and more aggressive, which is to say more moderate in each case. With such moderate rankings, take the opportunity to enhance or reduce certain characteristics by taking advantage of gender differences in behavior. You might want to increase the likelihood of demand for affection or acceptance of obedience training, or to reduce the tendency to fight with other dogs by selecting a female, or perhaps boost the drive toward territorial defense by choosing a male.

Weight: 75 pounds
Height: 26 inches
Build: Solid
Coat: Smooth
Color: Gray

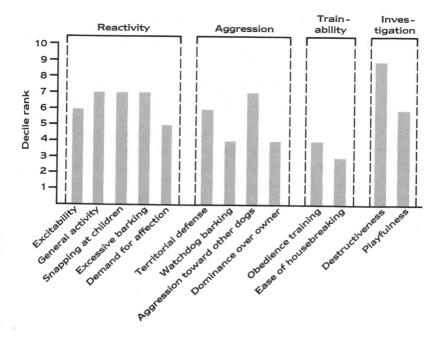

Welsh Corgi, Pembroke

The Welsh Corgi Pembroke may be just the dog for someone wanting a watchdog that also would be a nice family pet. The Corgi is unusual in that it has a quite manageable aggression profile. Its high ranking on aggressive traits includes high scores on the traits most related to territorial protection, but on the two traits more likely to contribute to problem behavior it ranks medium on aggression to dogs and low on dominance over owner.

The Corgi also ranks high on trainability, partially for its third-from-the-top ranking on ease of housebreaking. And it fulfills another family priority by combining high playfulness with low destructiveness. In overall reactivity the Corgi ranks medium, with no particularly high- or low-level traits. Thus, a family selecting this breed could expect an average amount of snapping at children and a low level of demand for affection. The Corgi's high ranking on training traits suggests that an owner could easily shape these traits as wanted.

No other breed has a profile quite like the Corgi's, particularly considering its modest size. It's like a smaller, more manageable, family version of the standard guard dogs in being as trainable as they are but not contesting for dominance over the owner as they might. The Corgi is also playful. The closest approach to the Corgi's profile is the Standard Poodle's. It is lower on overall aggression but still scores high on territorial defense and watchdog barking. The Collie and the Australian Shepherd have the same pattern of aggressive traits as the Corgi—the downward slope of characteristics visible on the graph. With any of these breeds, if you intend them to be watchdogs, select a male. If you'd like to reduce their tendency toward aggression, a female would be more suited to your needs.

Weight: 27 pounds
Height: 11 inches
Build: Average
Coat: Short
Color: Red, fawn,
    black and tan

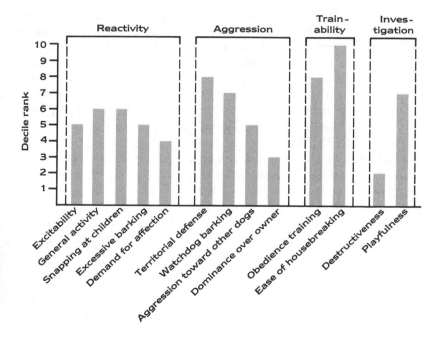

West Highland White Terrier

Devotees of the West Highland White Terrier probably enjoy its distinctive appearance and playfulness. Like virtually all terriers, the Westie can be counted on to be quite lively. In fact, this breed is one of the most reactive ones you'll find. Our authorities ranked it number one on general activity, two on excitability, and within the top few breeds on excessive barking and snapping at children. The West Highland White Terrier comes just behind the Miniature Schnauzer in setting the record for ranking extremely high on a majority of traits. Turn to the Miniature Schnauzer's profile, which may surprise you with its similarities. Some comments there about the Schnauzer thus apply equally well to the Westie.

Ranking within the top few breeds on watchdog barking and aggression toward other dogs, the Westie also ranks high on aggressive traits. Prospective owners should note the potential challenge of this breed, with its high levels of destructiveness and dominance over the owner combined with low trainability. Obedience-training sessions with a Westie might very well challenge the ingenuity and patience of owners who aren't assertive around dogs.

The West Highland White Terrier can be expected to serve you well for home protection, which may be reason enough to consider it as a pet. Keep in mind, though, that some good watchdog and territorial defender breeds do come with less aggression toward dogs and owners and with less reactivity. You might want to browse through the watchdog and territorial defense graphs in Part 2 again.

If you like the Westie's personality just as it is, you might want to check out the Fox Terrier. The primary difference between these breeds is the Fox Terrier's lower demand for affection and a drop in ease of training. If you're just looking for a little boost on obedience training, try the Miniature Schnauzer. And if the Westie's high aggression concerns you, the tiny Silky Terrier has only moderately high aggression and ranks medium on ease of training. Also recall that with these small dogs aggression can be a nuisance but lacks the possible serious consequences that can occur with larger breeds.

Weight: 16 pounds
Height: 11 inches
Build: Very light
Coat: Thick, hard,
  undercoat; regular
  grooming desirable;
  little shedding
Color: White

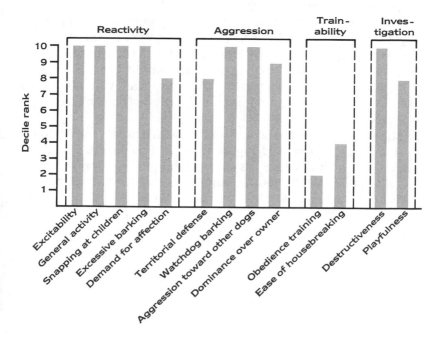

Yorkshire Terrier

The Yorkshire Terrier is a ball of fire in a tiny package, a minute dog that stands out on reactivity. The Yorkie ranks among the top few breeds on excitability, snapping at children, and excessive barking. For a tiny dog like this to get such high marks it must have really earned them. A limited aptitude for the trainability traits is part of the package.

There is considerable overlap among the many toy and terrier breeds, so you'd do well to review their similarities and differences and to recall that conformation and coat may often be the primary—or even sole—distinguishing characteristics between some breeds. In this area it often makes sense to choose finally from your short list of possibilities on the basis of looks or size.

The Yorkie's profile most closely corresponds to that of a larger dog, the West Highland White Terrier. The Yorkie ranks lower on aggressive traits, except for watchdog barking. The choice between these two breeds is probably made usually on the basis of the most obviously distinguishing characteristic, body size. A six-pound dog like the Yorkie can overwhelm you with its small size, which makes it a classic lap dog.

The Silky Terrier is another toy breed with a profile similar to the Yorkie's, but it is ranked higher in the trainability traits. If the Yorkie's high destructiveness and playfulness are drawbacks for you, the Chihuahua is another tiny breed that ranks low on these traits but is higher on aggressive characteristics.

Weight: 6 pounds
Height: 8 inches
Build: Fragile
Coat: Silky, long; regular
   grooming desirable;
   little shedding
Color: Blue with tan

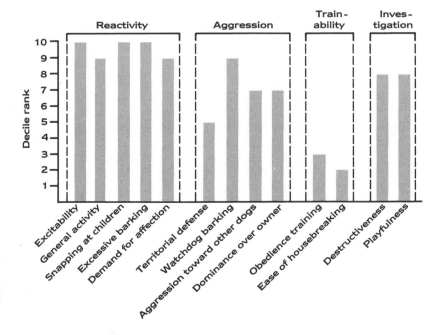

References

Arkow, P. S., and Dow S. "The ties that do not bind: A study of the human-animal bonds that fail." In R. K. Anderson, B. L. Hart, and L. A. Hart eds. *The Pet Connection: Its Influence on Our Health and Quality of Life.* Minneapolis: CENSHARE, 1984.

Clark, R. D., and J. R. Stainer. eds. *Medical and Genetic Aspects of Purebred Dogs.* Edwardsville, Kansas: Veterinary Medicine Publishing Co. 1983.

Hart, B. L., and L. A. Hart. "Selecting pet dogs on the basis of cluster analysis of breed behavioral profiles and gender." *Journal of the American Veterinary Medical Association,* 186, 1985a. pp. 1181–1185.

Hart, B. L., and L. A. Hart. *Canine and Feline Behavioral Therapy.* Philadelphia: Lea & Febiger, 1985b.

Hart, B. L., and M. F. Miller. "Behavioral profiles of dog breeds: A quantitative approach." *Journal of the American Veterinary Medical Association,* 186, 1985. pp. 1175–1180.

Hopkins, S. G., T. A. Schubert, and B. L. Hart. "Castration of adult male dogs: Effects on roaming, aggression, urine marking and mounting." *Journal of the American Veterinary Medical Association* 168, 1976. pp. 1108–1110.

Scott, J. P., and J. L. Fuller. *Genetics and the Social Behavior of the Dog.* Chicago: University of Chicago, 1965.

General Index

The pages on which the discussions and graphs of the thirteen key behavioral traits appear are shown in boldface.

Breed Index

The pages on which the fifty-six breed profiles appear are shown in boldface.